THIS BOOK IS DEDICATED TO
THE MEMORY OF
MARGARET WOODBURY STRONG (1897–1969).
HER FASCINATION WITH THE THINGS
OF EVERYDAY LIFE AND HER BENEVOLENCE
MADE THIS POSSIBLE.

CONTENTS

"The Light of Home," engraving From *Godey's Lady's Book*, July 1860.

The LIGHT of the HOME

AN INTIMATE VIEW OF THE LIVES OF WOMEN IN VICTORIAN AMERICA

HARVEY GREEN

WITH THE ASSISTANCE OF
MARY-ELLEN PERRY

WITH ILLUSTRATIONS FROM
THE MARGARET WOODBURY STRONG MUSEUM

PANTHEON BOOKS, NEW YORK

Library of Congress Cataloging in Publication Data

Green, Harvey, 1946–
The light of the home.

Includes index.
1. Women—United States—History—19th century.
2. Home economics—United States—History—19th century.
I. Perry, Mary-Ellen.   II. Title.
HQ1419.G73   1983   305.4′0973   82-18867
ISBN 0-394-71329-X

BOOK DESIGN BY SUSAN MITCHELL

Frontispiece, "The Light of Home"
1. Four studio portraits of young women
2. Combs and hairpins
3. Advertising poster for bicycles
4. Dance programs
5. Photograph album
6. Pencil drawing by young woman
7. Mechanical or "trick" valentine
8. "The Tap on the Window," plaster sculpture group
9. "Courtship," oil painting
10. Enameled porcelain dresser set
11. "Bride's bowl"
12. Photograph of home wedding
13. White silk wedding gown
14. Brown satin wedding gown
15. Bride's portrait photograph
16. Souvenir pincushion, sewing bird, and purse
17. Photograph of mother nursing twins
18. Glass and tin nursing bottles
19. Baby food advertising figurine and free samples
20. Advertising poster for Mellin's baby food
21. "Weighing the Baby," plaster sculpture group
22. Castor set
23. Magazine advertisement for child's corset
24. Chamber pot
25. Children's "teaching" plates
26. "Sunday" toys
27. Child's scrapbook of cut-out room interiors
28. Bliss doll houses
29. Toy stove, washer, and carpet sweeper
30. Child's sewing machine
31. Lady doll with papier-mâché head
32. Child dolls with bisque heads
33. Boy's toy locomotive
34. "Brownie" book, toy, and tableware
35. Pressed glass bread tray

Many people contributed to the preparation of this book. The board of trustees of the Margaret Woodbury Strong Museum and its two directors, Holman J. Swinney and William T. Alderson, have been committed from the outset to informing the public of the breadth and depth of United States history in the nineteenth century. Their continuing support in the preparation of this book cannot be overstated.

Mary-Ellen Earl Perry, curator of fine arts at the Strong Museum, provided nearly all of the research for chapters one, four, and six. She also located and assembled most of the artifactual materials illustrated in the book. Always cooperative, she carefully and diplomatically prevented me from pushing the evidence too far and kept my analyses closer to the things that real people used.

Many of her own family members, themselves products of the late Victorian era, contributed both information and support. The late Prudence Jamouneau and Mrs. Perry's parents, Sylvia A. and the late John H. Earl, were instrumental in her continued interest in the period. Most especially, Mrs. Perry wishes to thank her husband, Harold E. Perry, who never completely shared her enthusiasm for the late nineteenth century, but who appreciated hers and gave unfailing support even as he endured the subject morning, noon, and night for the years this project was under way.

Many people shared valuable information from their family records and reminiscences. Mary DeMund, Ruth B. Earl, Betty A. Lewis, William F. Sullivan, and Ruth Osborne Hill immeasurably aided this study.

Others on the museum staff gave support and encouragement, especially the chief librarian, Elaine Challacombe. She was always vigilant for the book or manuscript that would solve the problems that seemed monumental at the time. Mary Kay Ingenthron, director of public relations, and the museum's two photographers—Harry Bickelhaupt, who photographed the artifacts, and Tom Weber, who made the prints—were always willing to help whenever they could. Their work speaks for itself.

Sharon Allen typed the bulk of the manuscript and its revisions. She deserves special mention, not only for her competence as a translator of manuscript into typescript but also for her unfailingly pleasant disposition when confronted with an anxious writer trying to meet deadlines. We always got the job done.

Staff members at three other institutions were also helpful and encouraging. Alma Creek and Mary Huth of the rare books and manuscripts division of the University of Rochester Libraries were efficient and eager to help. The staff members at the New York Public Library and the Sophia Smith Collection at the Smith College Library answered my questions and located some wonderful materials for me.

Trudy Kramer, director of the Parrish Art Museum in Southampton, Long Island, introduced me and my work to André Schiffrin of Pantheon Books. Their continuing interest and support helped get this project under way. Wendy Wolf and Nan Graham of Pantheon were indispensable in the transformation of the manuscript into a publishable book. Candid, sensitive, and of the keenest of minds, they pressured, lectured, cajoled, and encouraged me in just the right ratio and at just the right times.

The manuscript itself never would have been written were it not for five other people. My parents, Herman and Bess Green, always encouraged me in my attempt to become an historian. They believed in me and in the importance of history when it would have been easy to criticize me for not entering a more "practical" profession.

I am also indebted to my mentor, Warren I. Susman. In his graduate seminars at Rutgers I began to learn this craft. He helped me see that cultural history embraces many disciplines. I am still learning to use all that he gave me.

All the hours of research, reading, painful organization, and still more difficult writing might have gone for nothing had it not been for Mary Lynn Stevens Heininger, the other half of the history department at the Strong Museum. Her incisive mind, editorial acumen, and contagious en-

Nearly every antique and curio shop in America has fragments of the everyday domestic life of the people who lived before us. If they are old enough, these trivets, mixing bowls, cups, saucers, and other household goods are endowed with the qualities of relics, to be purchased and lovingly displayed on mantels, shelves, or bookcases. What was once used to feed a family, nurse a child, clean and polish a teapot, or carry on the social graces and customs of another era has a different function in the present. These objects from the past suggest some sort of life that seems like ours but is foreign. Yet the common wares of the middle class in the late nineteenth century are more than decoration in the antique shops, museums, and homes of the 1980s; they are evidence of the customs and ideals of life in the domestic setting.

The purpose of this book is to understand the domestic lives of women in the late nineteenth century and the first decade of the twentieth century. In order to do that, it is necessary to examine not only what the protagonists read and the little that they wrote about their daily lives, but also the things with which they lived. In the latter half of the nineteenth century, American women could choose from a wide variety of books and pamphlets advising them about nearly all their household affairs. Often these words and ideas contradicted each other, or challenged traditional beliefs. Surviving artifacts of home life sometimes indicate that women chose the "old way" despite new advice. This is not to suggest that there is a consistent difference between advice and behavior; rather, the advice offered to women and the realities they faced in their attempts to achieve the ends desired of them could and did create tensions within their lives, and ultimately within the culture of the United States between 1870 and 1910.

The corsets and petticoats which have survived from this period make it clear that movement was difficult for women who dressed in fashion. But the cinched waist was more than simply uncomfortable; it was loaded with cultural meaning and information. In a society that valued display, restriction of movement was a signal that a woman did not have to endure the demanding physical labor of housework because her husband made enough money to pay for domestic help. Moreover, the restricted movement imposed by tightly laced corsets, metal stays, heavy petticoats, and high-heeled shoes was a kind of control over women. They paid the price of social censure if they rejected fashion for freer movement or participation in the male world.

Even those artifacts which seem to suggest the simple pleasures of life—a bicycle or a pair of ice skates—are symbols of a changing culture. Ice skating allowed courting couples the physical contact their society guarded against in most social situations. Bicycles made it possible for young people to find privacy—a scarce commodity in the cities and suburbs of turn-of-the-century America. They were also responsible, at least in part, for radical changes in women's dress.

I have decided to concentrate on middle-class women for two reasons. First, because they are part of the unexamined and vitally important mainstream of late-nineteenth-century American culture. Scholarly and popular analyses of exceptional women in America far outnumber studies of more typical women of the period. Second, I use as evidence the vast array of household objects that survive from the late nineteenth century. These objects were important in the everyday lives of the people who used them—women—and provide access to the regular cycles of daily activity often neglected by historians.

But if these artifacts have the appeal of authenticity, they also have the frustration of silence. Women usually used them with knowledge passed on to them orally by their mothers or other women. They seldom recorded the daily routines of their lives in a complete manner. I yearned for the perfect letter or diary that described in minute detail the comings and goings, the pains and pleasures, the joys and sorrows of life as it was. Even if such a spectacular source exists, it is probably suspect: Who wrote about everything they did? Why they are not *doing* it? If we are interested in the commonality of experience for the unexceptional members of society, then we must accept the fact that our information will be fragmented. Women of the late nineteenth century were not like the Puritans of seventeenth-century New England, anxiously keeping detailed diaries that might offer some hint of God's will toward their immortal souls. The great bulk of women's diaries of this period offer little information other than on weather conditions. But even if the references to family, work, leisure, personal well-being, and death are scattered, the patterns of thought about them are visible.

The advice literature in nineteenth-century America has been an important resource for this book. It is massive and, like the meticulously articulated diary, seductive. Reliance on advice literature alone as a key to behavior is a flawed methodology for two reasons. First, such a strategy leads as often to contradictions as it does to a clearer understanding, since these authors often disagreed. Second, etiquette book writers were often promoters of their own cause rather than accurate reporters of actual practices. In spite of these shortcomings, the patterns of response in their work can inform us about how individuals conducted themselves. This is especially true for the middle class, since advice manuals were most often aimed at them; the working classes were generally ignored, and the wealthy had the power, the station, and the tradition of family training in "proper behavior." The reality of everyday occurrences is often exactly what is most harshly criticized in the advice literature. Thus, criticism of the use of patent medicines and other crackpot nostrums for treatment of infant maladies suggests that in fact mothers loaded their young with alcohol and opium. Advertising ephemera from the period confirms this hypothesis. We can also surmise that dancing was a popular form of entertainment for women because so many advocates of propriety disapproved of it, arguing that it lured mothers away from their little ones.

The advice literature also helps reveal the larger cultural concerns of an era. John Harvey Kellogg, though an extremist in his attitudes about food and health, is informative because of the ways in which he couched his arguments. When he referred to the decline of American women from the allegedly sturdy grandmothers of the colonial days, he was not on the periphery of his culture, but squarely in the center of it. The sense that the United States had declined from an age of great men and women was constantly invoked in the later decades of the nineteenth century, and found expression in everything from domestic furnishings which replicated those of the eighteenth century to "colonial" brand carpet sweepers and cans of "pilgrim" strawberries.

I have also drawn on fiction—both novels and the short stories which appeared in the popular domestic magazines of the period—for information about women's lives in post–Civil War America. These works, like the advice books and articles of the era, usually present a moral lesson, or instruct the reader in the ways of society. The three most popular genres of literature—romance, death and consolation, and religion—illuminate not only the dreams and hopes of women (who constituted the majority of both the writers and the readers of fiction during this period) but also the standards by which they were urged to measure their lives.

Both women and men in turn-of-the-century America understood that their civilization was rapidly advancing. Material progress was occurring with startling rapidity. It offered the promise of comfort and respectability for those who succeeded, and a sense of personal failure for those who did not enjoy the fruits of prosperity. There were plenty of Americans living in the Northeast in 1870 who could easily remember the days when there were no railroads; now they lived in a nation that had been crossed by the rails. Thanks to the telegraph, they could read about the driving of the famous golden spike at Promontory Point, Utah, the day after it happened in 1869; with a little bit of luck, they might see an image of the event made by one of the many photographers peddling their wares.

By the late nineteenth century, the Northeast—the New England and Middle Atlantic states—was the most thoroughly industrialized and urbanized sector of the nation. By 1880 over one-half of the population lived in cities of over 8,000. Less than forty percent of the region's inhabitants were engaged in agriculture. They were forming what would become the typical family of late-nineteenth- to mid-twentieth-century America—father working outside the home, mother and children (fewer than there had been on the farm) in charge of the domestic realm. The sources I have relied on are those of the urban and village Northeast, the center of what I believe to be the domestic culture of the nation in the late nineteenth century.

The shifting of the workplace away from the home carried with it more subtle cultural changes. Women were sequestered from the so-called evils of commerce and production in homes where they were to be guardians of morality and cultivation, especially for their female children. Yet the comfort and status displayed in the home were inextricably linked to success in the marketplace, and it was an irresponsible mother who did not see to it that her male children were prepared for the competitive world of their father.

By the 1870s, however, there had been a revolution in American thinking about the nature of the pathway to success. Previous generations of Americans had identified material progress with morality, asserting, as did Edward Everett in 1826, that "the greatest engine of moral power . . . is an organized, prosperous state." Material well-being was a sign of God's grace; in the Protestant republic of the early nineteenth century, both the land and the people carried limitless potential. The two most important ministers of the middle decades of the century, Henry Ward Beecher and Horace Bushnell, affirmed this equation from the pulpit. Both were optimistic that the United States could easily absorb the best of other cultures, and that the dominant ethnic group—white Anglo-Saxon Protestants— would maintain its cultural and demographic hegemony. American men and women were as fertile as their land.

This racial-nationalist enthusiasm had its roots in literary and political speculation, rather than in scientific inquiry. The publication in 1859 of Charles Darwin's *On the Origin of Species by Means of Natural Selection, or the Preservation of Favored Races in the Struggle for Survival* (the full title of the work) changed everything. Learning about Darwin and social scientist Herbert Spencer's work in newspapers, at lectures, and in such popular scientific journals as E. L. Youman's *Popular Science Monthly,* Americans found great comfort in the idea of natural selection. Did not the very existence of their nation indicate that they were among the fittest?

The aggressive self-confidence of the immediate post–Civil War era was eroded, first by the severe economic depression of 1873–1878, and especially by the national railroad riots of 1877. The reality of burning railroad cars and pitched battles with state militias exacerbated fears among white Anglo-Saxons that their position of power was endangered. The popular press presented engravings, often on the front page, which graphically depicted a chaotic class war in the making. Railroad cars were shown ablaze; streetcars, tumbled on their sides to form barricades; policemen and strikers in combat. The violent strikes in the coal regions of Pennsylvania in the 1880s kept the threat of class conflict ever-present; the Haymarket bombings and the Knights of Labor strike of 1886, the bloody clashes at Homestead in 1892 and Pullman in 1894, and finally, the assassination of President McKinley by an eastern European "anarchist" in 1901 seemed to prove that WASP culture and hegemony were imperiled by immigrants "incapable of understanding our ideas and principles."[1]

Medicine and science were able to offer some explanations for these shocks to mainstream American culture. Physicians and scientists found disquieting information in American vital statistics: family size among urban and suburban WASPs was steadily declining, a trend that clearly endangered the demographic balance of power. Even more ominous, they saw the health of American men and women of the middle and upper classes deteriorating. Spiritual health alone was not sufficient; without physical vigor, the regenerate soul would be the last gasp of a dying race. Good health was essential for survival.

In the northeastern states, the late nineteenth century witnessed the passing of the traditions of American hand-craftsmanship and the rise to dominance of urban corporate capitalism. The roles of women and men in the family and in society became more distinct, and remained so until the 1960s. A woman born in 1870 might go through childhood, marry, raise her own family, and witness the death of her parents and some of her children by 1910. In those forty years she experienced the major rites of passage of a life. This book is about her life and other lives like hers. Probably no one woman experienced all of the cultural tensions and shocks of this period. Though the voices of individuals and their families are heard in the pages that follow, I was most interested in the pattern of women's response to and behavior in the world of the middle class in the nineteenth century. I became convinced that in their interpretations of their world and its changes, the men and women of the late nineteenth century laid the foundation for the building of modern American culture. Their concerns, fears, and expectations are very much our own.

"A WOMAN'S CALLING"

COURTSHIP AND MARRIAGE

1. Four studio portraits showing different poses and different degrees of informality. Tuttle and Company, Sodus, New York, c. 1889.

This is my birthday and the date of my martyrdom. Mother insists that at last I must have my hair "done up woman-fashion." My "back" hair is twisted up like a corkscrew; I carry eighteen hairpins; my head aches miserably; my feet are entangled in the skirt of my hateful new gown. I can never jump over a fence again, so long as I live.[1]

This is the reaction of Frances Elizabeth Willard, a founder of the Woman's Christian Temperance Union, to the sudden change in her life at the onset of puberty—the end of freedom. Like most prepubescent girls, she usually wore her hair unpinned and her dresses loose and hemmed well above her ankles (Figs. 1 and 2). The shock and anger that Willard felt was a counterpoint to the cultural imperative of marriage, to which a young woman was to aspire. With these changes in dress and hairstyle, a young woman was announced as one who would soon be available for courtship.

American society provided young women with numerous opportunities to meet eligible young men; one method was the system of "calling." A proper call, or visit, lasted no more than ten or fifteen minutes. If the person called upon was not home or unavailable, the caller left a personal card. The receiver of the card reciprocated with a call or a card if he or she desired to continue the social relationship. This formal procedure allowed people to communicate their social intentions without face-to-face interaction.

For unmarried women, the rules of calling were precise and strict. In some areas it was not considered correct for a young lady to have cards of her own during her first year in "society." Instead, her name was printed beneath her mother's name on her mother's card. In the middle of the nineteenth century, the title "Miss" on the card was not allowed young women: only older unmarried women were permitted to use it. By the 1880s etiquette books stated that the title was to be used on the cards of all unmarried women, a change which suggests that the title

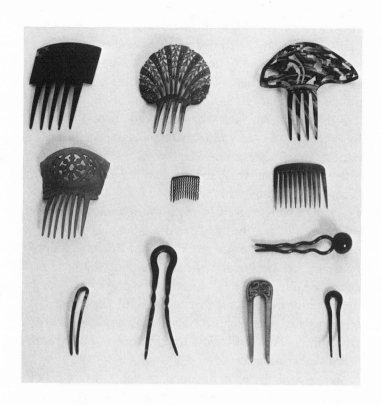

2. Women commonly used several combs and
hairpins to keep their hair in place.
Tortoise shell, plastic, and silver. American,
1870–1910.

3. Bicycles allowed courting couples to get away from the watchful eyes of family and neighbors, as they have in this advertising poster. Strobridge Lithograph Company, Cincinnati, Ohio, c. 1896.

FOR HEALTH & RECREATION
RIDE A CRAWFORD BICYCLE
$60 NONE BETTER $75
FEW AS GOOD

became more an indication of marital status, and less a sign of the prestige afforded to older women.[2]

Flirting was socially acceptable as a way for a young woman to reveal her social grace and her availability to prospective suitors. *Godey's Lady's Book* explained: "Flirting is to marriage what free trade is to commerce. By it the value of a woman is exhibited, tested, her capacities known, her temper displayed, and the opportunity offered of judging what sort of a wife she may probably become."[3] Although this suggests that a woman was passively marketing herself to men, much as a horse-trader sold a race horse, flirting offered a woman some control over her situation. Since she could not properly propose marriage, her only real choice was among the men who expressed interest in her. Flirtatious behavior gave her the opportunity to broaden that network of eligible and interesting men, enabling her to make a wiser choice about which man she would allow to court her and which proposal she would accept.

Sixteen was the recommended age for a young lady to begin to keep company with young men, although courting as early as fourteen was acceptable. In England in the 1870s and 1880s, "respectable girls" had chaperones for most activities, but chaperones were rarer in American social life of the same period. Here, unchaperoned social activity was the norm, and young people had more social freedom than their English counterparts. Courting couples attended social affairs with young married friends rather than with older women. The greater freedom in America was in part the result of the less rigid class structure of the United States and, in part, of the less secure and respected position of older single women in American culture.

New leisure activities in the late nineteenth century became valuable opportunities for courtship. Roller and ice skating gave young couples the chance to hold hands in public, and bicycles gave couples a chance to be alone together (Fig. 3). By the late 1890s it was acceptable for a couple to sit by themselves behind closed doors in the parlor, or to go to the Adirondacks and other relatively remote places with other couples. Spending their days together hiking and climbing, men and women slept either in separate cabins or on opposite sides of the same cabin. Young married couples went along as guardians of proper behavior.

Music was an important part of Victorian courtship, and the ability to play the piano was a special asset for courting couples. They could sit at the piano together, playing duets published especially for the amateur market. Many of these songs called for the players' hands to cross over, thus providing another opportunity for touching and privacy within the confines of the home's most public space, the parlor.[4]

Dances and balls were popular among courting couples, in spite of the fulminations of reformers and critics who thought that such amusements would distract young women from discharging their family responsibilities. Critics who worried about the "fleeting and unsubstantial pleasures of the ball room"[5] did not find a sympathetic audience with men and women who wanted the physical closeness and private conversation dancing provided. When she arrived at the dance, each young woman received a program on which young men signed up for the various dances (Fig. 4). The successful social strategist filled her program at the start of the evening with men she liked, but she never danced more than two dances with one man, lest she incite gossip. This was a risky business; if she refused others, hoping that her favorites would ask, she chanced becoming a wallflower. By allowing the first men who asked to sign her program, a young woman might have no room left when her favorites did appear. Yet an unanticipated opening on her program was considered embarrassing. Cutting or refusing to dance with someone once his name was on the program was not considered proper unless the man had behaved badly or had paid undue attention to another woman during the evening. The initiative in this situation was quite clearly with men, but the environment allowed women to find privacy with

4. These dance programs not only illustrate the formalized nature of activities at dances; they also show the number of different dances men and women were expected to know. Paper and cotton cord. American, 1885–1911.

men they favored and to limit the attentions of men for whom they did not care.

When courting, a lady was never to take a gentleman's arm unless he offered it. It was improper for a gentleman to offer his arm during the day, unless they were engaged. After dark or in places where footing was unsure, it was acceptable for a man to offer his arm to the woman he was escorting whether or not they were engaged. Protracted "good nights" were improper; a young woman was to stand outside her home with her escort no longer than five minutes. If it was still early evening when they got home, she could ask him in, but he was not to stay longer than half an hour.

In making their departure, couples were supposed to address each other formally. The use of first names was acceptable only for those who had known each other since childhood. For those who met as adults, the use of the prefix "Mister" or "Miss" was standard. In 1889, when asked if it was proper for a young man to ask a young woman to address him by his Christian name at their first meeting, M. S. Logan's answer in *The Home Manual* was: "Certainly not. It would be a great presumption."[6]

The proper gifts for a young man to give a young lady when calling on her were flowers, candy, or a book (Fig. 5). Because flowers and candy were perishable, no undue significance was attached to them. In 1870 the editors of *Godey's* stated: "It is not customary to give presents unless the parties are engaged."[7] This principle was probably ignored; one month later, the same magazine conceded that a woman could accept gifts of trifling value from a man to whom she had been introduced. The reasoning behind this apparent contradiction was that it was better to accept such offerings gracefully than to decline them: refusal suggested that the woman attached more importance to the gifts than the man meant to convey.

A proper young woman could not offer a man a gift until he had given one to her. Women were to be content with simply wishing men a "Merry Christmas" or sending birthday greetings. The *Woman's Home Companion* of

A present to Miss Julia S. Sell, from Dr. Joseph Sullens.

November 1899 advised: "A cordial letter of kind wishes sent to arrive on your friend's birthday would be sufficient to express your remembrance and good-will."[8] Once a man had initiated an exchange of gifts, a young woman was free to reciprocate, within established canons of taste. Ideally, such gifts were to be delicate, artistic, handmade, and inexpensive. A pencil drawing (Fig. 6) or "a trifle from your needle" was acceptable.

In the late nineteenth century, valentines, like calling cards, could be a vehicle for the hopeful courter. Elaborate valentines, often imported from Germany, were frequently used to express a deeper emotional involvement. The most popular were known as "trick" or "mechanical" valentines: the flat card opened to become a standing model, replete with cupids, doves, hearts, flowers, and sentimental messages (Fig. 7).

Victorian lovers were urged to remember the practical

5. Albums and commemorative books were particularly popular gifts during this period. Photograph album, velvet, paper, and brass. American, c. 1892.

6. This pencil drawing would have been a suitable gift from the young woman who made it to her suitor. American, c. 1850.

facet of marriage, and to consider both the mental and physical health of their potential mate. Both men and women (or their fathers on their behalf) were urged to consult the family doctor of their lover before proposing or accepting a proposal. Doctors, writers, and clergymen frequently addressed young men, warning them that women were delicate and more susceptible than men to mental illness. If there was any taint of insanity or physical disability in the family history of the prospective spouse, the other lover could end the relationship before it was made public.[9] Financially and socially successful families feared for their future in a country becoming more densely populated, both with "suspect" immigrants and with established citizens who seemed to represent a decline from the allegedly strong founders of the country. This sense of degeneration was presented by laymen and ministers in popular magazines and such books as the Reverend John

Ellis' *The Deterioration of the Puritan Stock and Its Causes* (1884). Ellis' pessimistic interpretation remained popular until the 1920s, and is perhaps the most lucid synthesis of the conservative clerical response to immigration and changing American mores.

Men had the responsibility of proposing marriage. The most proper way to propose was in person (Fig. 8), but a proposal by letter was acceptable. If the right man proposed marriage, a lady was not to respond in a falsely modest or coy manner. In a letter printed in the March 1870 issue of *Godey's Lady's Book,* three young women asked how often a man's proposal of marriage should be refused before being accepted. The editors bluntly stated that such a question was "stupid," and maintained that if a young woman intended to accept a proposal she should do so when first asked: a true lady did not play with a man's affections. If a woman rejected a proposal, she was expected to explain her decision to the spurned suitor, and she was socially bound to speak about it only with her parents.[10]

Parents who disapproved of the man to whom their daughter became engaged were urged to work indirectly to change their daughter's mind. Finding a more suitable man to distract her often succeeded where direct opposition failed. Another recommended tactic was to point out unobtrusively the objectionable traits of the suitor, with the hope that the young woman would independently decide to end the relationship. If neither of these methods worked, parents who could afford to sent their daughter away, either to travel or to visit family or friends. Young women went on these trips, however unwillingly, because they had no other option. With virtually no economic opportunities in the outside world, the single, middle-class woman was dependent on her parents for her survival.

If her parents liked him and she had accepted his proposal, the prospective groom was then to speak to his fiancée's father and request consent to marry. At this meeting, the would-be husband was to outline his financial expectations. Here was a confrontation between genera-

7. Most mechanical or "trick" valentines were made in Europe. More expensive than plain lithographed or printed pieces, these valentines were, for the middle class, emblems of a special relationship. Cut and lithographed paper. German, 1895–1905.

8. This humorous sculpture group depicts not only the proper way for a young man to propose to his beloved but also the trappings of the proper young woman. The table is a sewing table, indicating her domestic talents, and he has brought her flowers. "The Tap on the Window," painted cast plaster. John Rogers and Company, New York, c. 1870.

tions and genders; the young man seeking permission from the patriarch, and the young woman subordinate to both her father and her proposed mate. A father could demonstrate his power by delaying the wedding plans if he felt any uncertainty about the match. Fiction in ladies' magazines often emphasized the tragic effects of such delays. The December 1870 issue of *Godey's* carried a story that told of the unhappy consequences of parental interference. Believing their son too young and wild to undertake the responsibilities of marriage, the young man's family prevented the proposed alliance. Two years later, an epidemic brought him close to death. His grief-stricken parents sent for his former love and the young man died in her arms. True to his memory, the young woman never married but instead devoted herself to her orphaned young nephews and nieces.[11] For women readers of the late nineteenth century, this theme functioned as solace, warning, or comfort. Fiction revealed the power structure of the family, and provided a means of coping with the reality of a woman's subordination to father and fiancé.

Before she became engaged, a woman answered to her father for most of her actions; once betrothed, that power passed to her fiancé. He was expected to call on her every evening (Fig. 9), and she could no longer receive evening visits from former admirers. Once her engagement was announced a woman was expected to discontinue private correspondence with other men, unless her fiancé approved.

The middle-class token of engagement was a ring. According to *Demorest's Monthly Magazine*, in the 1870s popular ring types included "handsome pearl or solitaire diamond rings"; a diamond, ruby, and sapphire combination setting; and an amethyst ring with a monogram set in small "brilliants." It was acceptable for men whose means were limited to offer a flat gold band as an engagement ring. This ring was worn on the third finger of the right hand until the wedding; then it was transferred to the left hand to accompany the wedding band. The proper wedding band for a Victorian bride was always of "plain, heavy gold." In 1870 readers of *Godey's* were informed that "gentlemen sometimes wear engagement rings, but not often." Nor did men commonly wear wedding bands.[12]

To announce their engagement, the proper couple wrote personal notes to their friends or told them in person. Close relatives and friends who lived far away were to be written at the same time so that they would not be hurt by hearing the important news secondhand. Once the engagement had been announced, the man's family was expected to welcome the woman promptly and cordially. In February 1864, a young woman wrote to her parents telling them how her fiancé's family reacted when they learned of the

9. Courting commonly took place in the home of the woman, usually not far from mother's watchful eyes or sharp ears. "Courtship," oil on canvas, artist unknown. American, c. 1870.

couple's engagement. Her mother wrote back: "The kind and loving welcome accorded you by his family is gratifying to us, and must be very pleasing to you."[13] In many cities it was customary for the man's family to invite their son's fiancée and her family to dinner soon after the engagement was made public, thereby giving the match an official seal of approval. Families might also show their approval of the engagement by giving a formal reception in honor of the couple.

Personal circumstances determined the length of Victorian engagements. Urged to wait until they had sufficient money to live independently, couples were nonetheless advised to avoid long engagements. "They are universally embarrassing and dangerous. Lovers are so apt to find out each other's imperfections, to grow exacting, jealous, and morose."[14] Long periods of betrothal were also opposed because the inevitable increase in intimacy might lead to sexual involvement and pregnancy. Women were taught that their chastity was their choicest possession: "To keep a man's love you must keep his respect." They were warned that an engagement was not marriage and that during their engagement they should be on their guard at all times. "Think of the difference between a promise of marriage and an actual marriage itself. There must be no rough freedom, no romping caresses, no behavior that you would be ashamed of if the engagement should be broken."[15]

If circumstances necessitated breaking an engagement, the reasons for the termination were to be stated in a letter. Sent with the letter were all portraits, letters, or gifts that had been received during the engagement. The recipient of the termination letter was to reply in a dignified manner without attempting to change the partner's mind unless "he or she is greatly mistaken in his or her premises."[16] The rejected person was also to return all gifts. To avoid awkward meetings, couples were advised to stay away from social events after the engagement was broken.

Nineteenth-century domestic advisors disagreed about the proper age for marriage. Some urged early marriage as the best way to perpetuate the species. Others advised that early marriage was hazardous for young women because "premature love robbed the nerve and brain of their natural needs and blighted the organs of sex."[17] The average age of a woman who married in the 1890s was twenty-two; her counterpart of the 1790s married when she was twenty-seven. The trend toward younger brides was probably the result of lessened family demands in an urban industrial culture, rather than a response to domestic advisors.[18]

American women were urged to postpone marriage until they were in their twenties, but they were warned not to wait until they reached "the shady side of thirty." As D. Dora Nickerson remarked in *The Household*: "If a woman is thirty and unmarried, men straightaway question for the reason, and then seek no farther [*sic*] acquaintance because someone hasn't made the Miss a Mrs. before."[19] The popular suspicion was that such a woman had a difficult temperament which would make her undesirable in a family. Yet young women were also warned not to accept any man, just to be married. They were reminded that life as an "old maid" could be rewarding and useful, and was preferable to marrying without love.

Courtship was, ironically, a threat to the happiness of women once they married. Traditional courting behavior raised the expectations of women, who thought that their suitors' attention and submission would continue after marriage. Families and domestic advisors tried to prepare young women for the shock of the end of the honeymoon. One mother wrote to her young daughter that "the devotion of the lover seldom survives the bridal, but where the wife has cultivated those qualities which will command lasting regard and esteem, there comes a quiet happiness, far more enduring."[20] The husband's obligation was to love and cherish his wife, but this behavior was paradoxically linked to her willingness to submit to him cheerfully in all areas of life. For women who wondered why the roles could not sometimes be reversed, the standard answer was a tautology: Only a "henpecked" man would accept a role reversal, and the true-spirited woman "would blush to acknowledge herself the wife of such a dastardly man as would submit to such treatment."[21]

In spite of these contradictions, the young Victorian woman had high expectations of marriage. It was a woman's great adventure, filled with possibilities and risks.

Once a couple decided to marry and obtained their parents' approval, they chose the date, usually a weekday or a Sunday rather than a Saturday. Saturday was considered an unlucky day for a wedding.

> *Monday for wealth,*
> *Tuesday for health,*
> *Wednesday the best day of all;*
> *Thursday for losses,*
> *Friday for crosses,*
> *And Saturday no luck at all.*[22]

Verbal invitations—with printed announcements following the ceremony—were proper for small weddings. For those choosing to send printed invitations, etiquette books prescribed the proper form: six and one-half by four and one-quarter inches, with a restrained typeface (neither Old English nor German Script) on satin-finish paper. As M. S. Logan intoned in *The Home Manual*: "Under no circumstances allow your friends or your stationer to persuade you to use a fancy paper or type; the envelope should match the paper exactly, and should be perfectly plain, with a long pointed flap, and without gum."[23]

A wedding invitation was an indication to the recipient that the married couple wished to continue their social relationship, and it obligated the recipient to provide a gift (Figs. 10 and 11). In 1909 Laura Osborne of Rochester, New York, selected gifts for three of her children to send to their brother, who was getting married. For the two younger children, she chose two silver saltcellars and, for her older daughter, she bought "a pretty green and white small teapot." For her own wedding in 1881, Laura had

received three books of poetry and several paintings, including a large reproduction of Sir Joshua Reynolds' *Choir of Angels,* another of St. Cecile, "a panel picture of pansies," and a picture of "roses painted in oil on china plaque." The latter two were probably hand-painted by friends. The offer of a family heirloom was a symbol of trust. Fifty-four years after she had received them, Almira MacDonald, Laura Osborne's mother, sent her granddaughter-in-law, Lura Cooley Osborne, "two of my 1855 wedding tablespoons as a gift." The following day she received "a long, lovely letter from Lura with regard to my gift for them."[24]

In an article in *Godey's,* Henry Ward Beecher argued that rather than giving practical and useful items to help a young couple set up housekeeping, people were more concerned with exhibiting their own status with their gifts. According to Beecher, the custom of displaying wedding gifts on the day of the marriage had helped promote this attitude, and he criticized those who gave beyond their means. Deeming such motives offensive, the editors of *Godey's* criticized the practice of giving wedding gifts, and were pleased to report in the March 1870 issue that they

13. A typical nineteenth-century white wedding gown, which would not ordinarily have been worn again for any other function. Ivory silk faille, Valenciennes lace, and pearls. L. P. Hollander and Company, Boston, c. 1885.

had produced some results: "It is not uncommon now to see on wedding cards, 'No presents received.' " Yet Beecher's and the magazine's crusade against ostentatious gifts had little long-term effect. In the January 1873 issue, the editors noted with disapproval: "Wedding cards are now issued with the notice, 'No plated ware' printed in one corner."[25]

The manner in which a home was decorated for a wedding or reception emphasized the special nature of the day and reinforced the idea that the marriage rite was the beginning of the bride and groom's responsibility to form a home and family (Fig. 12). The household furnishings, many familiar to the bride since childhood, were commonly adorned with flowers and greenery, symbols of the God-given interdependence of the natural world. For Lura Cooley Osborne's reception:

The rooms . . . were decorated with ferns and flowers; a large palm at end of hall and high vases of roses at front entrance. At top of stairs in the turn stood a large palm. The front drawing room mantel had banks of daisies and ferns—the fireplace filled with ferns. . . . The sitting room with palms against the long mirror, mahogany table against it with large glass punch bowl and glasses—high bouquets on mantel. The music room and room back of it, bouquets of roses. The dining room, above the sideboard . . . with candles burning in front and vases of pink clover blossoms. From the dome over the table, festoons of pink clover blossoms.[26]

The ornamenting of everyday artifacts—tables, mantels, étagères—with symbol-laden floral decoration transformed the familiar home into an extraordinary garden. Full of the beauty and innocence of nature, the parlor was still home, the symbol of the family. Special music, played on pianos and organs, emphasized the connection between home and church. Conflict must have arisen within the bride: the familiar setting of her home was made glorious, just as she was abandoning it. The wedding and reception in the home were symbolic transferences from the bride's "center" of innocence and maidenhood to a new "center" in which she was to assume the role of nurturer.

White, symbolizing purity and virginity, has become the traditional color for the wedding dress. In the late nineteenth century, however, many women chose colored dresses in which to be married. These dresses could then be reused for other social events. Maude Heath of Gloversville, New York, for example, wore a white Brussels lace and net dress for her marriage to Dudley Wilcox in 1906 (Fig. 13), but Ada Jamouneau of Newark, New Jersey, wore a brown satin wedding dress (Fig. 14).[27] The qualities of chastity and fertility were embodied in the bouquet carried by the bride. Since the orange tree bears flowers and fruit simultaneously, its blossoms were the favorite flower for brides. Bridesmaids were emblematic of the world the bride was leaving, and therefore were supposed to be unmarried and younger than the bride.

The formal bridal portrait was less important as a record of the Victorian wedding than it is today. Women who wanted formal portraits usually were photographed some time after the wedding (Fig. 15). Laura Osborne of Victor, New York, went with her mother to the photographer's

14. This wedding gown indicates that in the nineteenth century, white was not the only acceptable color for a nuptial gown. It was probably worn after the ceremony for special occasions. Brown satin with faceted metal buttons. American, 1889.

15. Wedding portraits became fashionable in the 1870s, as photography became cheap and widely practiced. This wedding portrait was taken about one year after the ceremony: it was the bride, not the ceremony, who was commemorated. Langtry Studios, American, c. 1875–1890.

studio more than two months after her wedding; Maude Wilcox was photographed in her bridal gown the year following her wedding, but without the veil she had worn for the actual ceremony.[28] The popularity of the new Kodak camera resulted in a proliferation of informal wedding photographs, and these images illuminate the complex set of expectations and lost innocence of the wedding.

New possibilities for middle-class honeymooners were introduced by the network of rail transportation that covered the Northeast by the 1870s. Rail travel was faster and less arduous than the carriages or coaches of the past, and the railroads helped spawn a new institution—the honeymoon resort. Saratoga, the White Mountains, and Niagara Falls were extremely popular among honeymoon couples, and some hotels even greeted guests with a burst of band music as their carriage drew up to the hotel portico. Small gift shops and bazaars abounded in such resorts, catering to the visitors' desire for souvenirs, such as feathered fans, miniature bark canoes, jewelry and vases carved from local rocks, or Indian beadwork (Fig. 16). The souvenir became part of the American domestic landscape.

Brides were advised to camouflage their newlywed status on their honeymoons. In William Dean Howells' *Their Wedding Journey,* Isabel, a twenty-seven-year-old bride, nervously asked her husband: "We shall not strike the public as bridal, shall we? My one horror in life is an evident bride." When Maude and Dudley Wilcox arrived at their hotel in Niagara Falls, they very carefully spread newspapers over the floor of their room before changing from their traveling clothes. The paper would catch any stray grains of rice which might betray their newly married status to the hotel staff. Public displays of affection were condemned by the authors of etiquette manuals as expressions of the "common" people. "Avoid, as intensely vulgar, any display of your position as a bride, whilst traveling," wrote Florence Hartley in *The Ladies' Book of Etiquette and Manual of Politeness* (first published in 1860).[29] Members of the predominantly Protestant middle class believed that control of passion would distinguish them from the working class and the new, generally Roman Catholic, immigrants from southern and eastern Europe. The rules of decorum helped maintain class distinctions.

The affected sophistication of the newlywed couple also masked sexual naiveté. Since discussion of sexuality was virtually nonexistent in the schooling and upbringing of young women, most of them were sexually ignorant when they married. But the sexual inexperience of a bride was inappropriate for the woman who suddenly had the responsibilities of a wife. The middle-class bride experienced a public ritual but not a private initiation into the mysteries of womanhood. Expected to be pure and innocent until her wedding day, the bride was supposed to be transformed instantly into a wise childbearer familiar with the actuality of sexual relations and pregnancy. Her only preparation was her new title "Mrs."

When the newlyweds returned from their wedding trip, it was customary for the groom's family to give them a reception, and for members of both families to give dinner parties in their honor.[30] Bridesmaids and wedding guests also entertained the newlyweds sometime during the winter season following the wedding. At a formal ball or dinner party, it was appropriate for the bride to wear her wedding gown, without the orange blossoms and veil.

The new bride was expected to hold several receptions or teas for the people she wished to retain as friends. A bride might enclose an "at home" card, stating the days and hours during which she would receive guests, with her wedding invitations, or she might issue her cards after her trip. If a woman's husband could not be with her to receive their guests, her mother, sister, or a friend was asked to be present.

"At once the absolute mistress of her own heart, and the molder, purifier, and uplifter of him she glorifies with her love," a bride was expected to conduct herself with modesty and propriety to uphold her husband's name.[31] The foremost responsibility of a new wife was to provide for her husband "a happy home . . . the single spot of

16. Souvenirs became part of the American landscape in the late nineteenth century. Inexpensive triggers to the memory, they were popular among honeymooners and other travelers. Pincushion, bird, and purse, polished cotton and glass beads. American, c. 1900–1905.

rest which a man has upon this earth for the cultivation of his noblest sensibilities."[32] The rudiments of this responsibility—selecting and arranging furniture, decorating the house, cooking, cleaning, and doing laundry—were central not only to her husband's contentment, but also to her preparation for her ultimate purpose: bearing and raising children.

"The foundation of our national character," wrote Josiah Gilbert Holland ("Timothy Titcomb") in 1858, "is laid by the mothers of the nation."[1] Holland was probably the most popular nonministerial writer about family life in the latter half of the nineteenth century. In hundreds of articles throughout the popular press and scores of inexpensive books, Holland argued that motherhood was the role toward which a woman's life was directed. In post–Civil War America, bearing children allegedly made women healthier, avoided complications in menopause, and, as Holland implied, assured the continuation of the hegemony of white Anglo-Saxon Protestant Americans in an age of labor violence, economic dislocation, and massive immigration from Roman Catholic Europe.

Holland further argued that children were an essential component in a proper marriage because they enabled women to "reach the highest and most harmonious development of which [they] are capable. Without [children], one of the most beautiful regions of [a woman's] nature must forever remain without appropriate and direct culture. . . . [Children] make us tender and sympathetic, and a thousand times reward us for all we do for them." Pregnancy and motherhood were also characterized as beneficial to women's physical development. A columnist in *Demorest's Monthly Magazine* wrote that "bearing children tends to keep beauty of form and feature—other things being equal—even increasing it sometimes, and putting old age a long way off." Motherhood, contended the editors of *Godey's Lady's Book,* was the most "striking and beautiful" aspect of the "female character," providing the "fulfillment of a woman's physiological and moral destiny."[2]

A woman who neglected this ordained purpose was denying herself an opportunity for physical and moral development. According to H. S. Pomeroy, whose *Ethics of Marriage* was first published in 1888, childless women also faced a greater chance of disease than did mothers. He specifically pointed to menopause, a period in a woman's life during which he was certain cancer of the repro-

TWO

MADONNA in the NURSERY

THE CULT OF MOTHERHOOD

ductive system was a great risk.[3] This was an especially threatening disclosure for young women because they were socialized to anticipate the "change of life" with fear, just as they had been warned about puberty.[4]

The stridency with which these critics promoted the benefits of childbirth and the dangers of failing to conceive is directly linked to the very real threat to women's lives that birth held. In an era when most births occurred at home, with other women relatives and friends present, most women saw the pain and frequent death caused by childbirth. But children, wrote Holland, were "cheap at the price of pain and sickness."

The domestic advisors, physicians, and other moral reformers who admonished women about their responsibility to bear children became more fervent in the three decades preceding 1900. Critics were aware of the declining birthrate of white Anglo-Saxon families during the nineteenth century: for white women between fifteen and forty-four years old, the birthrate dropped from 278 live births per 1,000 women in 1800 to 124 live births per 1,000 in 1900 (Fig. 17).[5] Average family size decreased from seven (5 children) in 1800 to between five and six (3.42 children) in 1910.[6] The drop in the birthrate among white middle-class women and the simultaneous immigration of large numbers of allegedly fertile southern and eastern European women threatened the stability of the existing social order of late-nineteenth-century America. If the "good native stock" of America continued to have smaller families than the immigrants, who would rule?

Cultural critics blamed apartment living, contraception, and abortion for the declining birthrate. Abortions were inexpensive and common in the late nineteenth century: ten dollars was a standard rate in New York and Boston; and in 1898 the Michigan Board of Health estimated that one-third of all pregnancies were artificially terminated.[7] The availability of abortion and contraceptive devices may not have actually increased between 1870 and 1900, but the published outcry against them indicates a growing cultural concern. Holland condemned the "great and growing

vice among the young married people of this country—a vice which involves essential murder in many instances, and swells the profits of a thousand nostrum vendors."[8]

Abortifacients could be purchased through the mail, and were quietly promoted in the magazines and books of the period. "Monsieur Desmoreaux's Preventive to Conception," for example, was advertised in Dr. A. M. Mauriceau's *The Married Women's Private Medical Companion*, a long and detailed treatise in favor of birth control, which detailed horrors of Caesarian "butchery," prostitution, poverty, promiscuity among men, and propagation of the lesser intellects of the species. Mauriceau was the sole American agent for the patent medicine contraceptive, which "neutralized the fecundating properties of semen." For ten dollars, he guaranteed that "the packages can be forwarded to all parts of the United States."[9]

The argument against family limitation and childless marriages went beyond arguments for racial or national preservation. Children were an expression of the era's moral equation of intercourse and procreation. Sex without reproduction was immoral. Holland had characterized the woman who, "by cool and calculating choice, is no mother . . . [as] either very unfortunately organized, or . . . essentially immoral." Half a century later, Mary Wood-Allen, a physician in charge of the Purity Department of the Woman's Christian Temperance Union, similarly snarled: "If she purposes deliberately to avoid motherhood she puts herself in a position of moral peril, for such immunity is not often secured except at the risk of criminality. . . . All attempts to secure the pleasure of a physical relation and escape its legitimate results are a menace to the health and a degradation to the moral nature."[10]

The decline of the birthrate at the turn of the century is quite extraordinary given popular knowledge about conception cycles. Many physicians and popular health advisors were certain that conception occurred just before menstruation, and that is what they told their patients and readers. As Wood-Allen explained: "The uterus is lined by a mucous membrane similar to that which lines the mouth, and at the time of ovulation this membrane becomes swollen and soft, and little hemorrhages, or bleedings, occur for three or four days; the blood passing away through the vagina. This is called menstruation."[11]

Women who did not know about birth control, or did not believe in it, probably felt safe having intercourse with their husbands or lovers precisely when they were most likely to become pregnant. Moreover, a couple wishing to limit conception might have practiced withdrawal just before menstruation, but not in the middle of the cycle, prompting what Mauriceau termed "unjust and unfounded suspicions." Misinformation bewildered women about their physiology, and made them susceptible to irrational explanations for pregnancy or for their inability to conceive. The confusion might also have convinced men and women that there was only one sure way to avoid pregnancy—abstinence. For critics of contraception, the model wife was someone like Susan Huntington Hooker of Rochester, New York, who in 1872 wrote her sister: "Mother said that she did not know whether she had mentioned the fact that we have another son. Such a common occurrence that it is no novelty."[12] She bore eight children.

During pregnancy, women were supposed to exercise extreme care, since they were allegedly weakened by their condition. Most marriage manuals forbade intercourse during pregnancy because it would harm the fetus. Women were urged to consider themselves "gardeners" whose duty it was to provide "good soil" for the baby. They were advised to stop wearing corsets, to avoid the "alcoholic and tobacco exhalations" of their spouses, and to be physically active, even if their state embarrassed them.[13] In an article in *The Household*, a magazine published in Brattleboro, Vermont, an anonymous columnist maintained: "Walking is decidedly useful and no false modesty should prevent a woman from going out freely for the exercise she so much needs. If she respects herself, she will have the respect of all decent people. . . . Of course a modest woman does not needlessly publish her sacred secret."[14] Pregnancy was an ambiguous state. It affirmed the woman as successfully performing her most important role as a wife, but it also made public the private ritual of sexual intercourse.

Two contradictory approaches to pregnancy underlie the obstetrical literature and practice of the nineteenth century. Some physicians and advisors considered pregnancy and childbirth part of a natural physiological process, and favored "waiting on nature" for delivery; others viewed pregnancy as a "disease" which required vigorous intervention—the use of forceps and drugs, and the confinement of women to hospitals. Instrument deliveries, according to historians Regina Morantz and Sue Zschoche, apparently increased in the late nineteenth century, and some contemporary physicians purported that the change was necessary because women had been weakened by the effects of urban life.[15] It may also have been due to physicians' eagerness to use technology to control nature—in this case, women's bodies.

Once a child had been safely delivered, there was plenty of advice on feeding, clothing, exercise, and proper training for the infant. Neglect was unconscionable, and, as a short story in *Godey's* warned in 1860, could lead to the death of the infant. The protagonist in the story left her son Willie for the temptations of "the world of fashion of which [her] gay friends formed a part." She was an "unfaithful mother," and during her "winter of dissipation," her son became ill. Having left him again for a "tableau party," she was summoned to his bedside, as he lay dying. The tale ends with a soliloquy by the woman, chastened by her loss, but fortunate to have another child to raise.[16]

Nurturing has always been significant because the child is the key to the future. But the methods of nurturing changed dramatically during the Enlightenment in accord with new attitudes toward children. In *The Nature of Early Piety* (1721), clergyman Benjamin Wadsworth asserted that children are the "meer nest, root, [and] fountain of Sin, and wickedness. . . . Indeed, as sharers in the guilt of *Adam's* first sin, they are *Children of Wrath* by Nature, liable to eternal Vengeance, the Unquenchable Flames of Hell."[17] Ideas about children changed about 1800 as part of the broad cultural and intellectual impact of the Enlightenment, with its faith in reason and human potential. Unitarians, specifically William Ellery Channing, publicly rejected the theory of infant damnation in 1809; Lyman Beecher dismissed the idea of inherent evil in 1828.

Post-Enlightenment optimism about the nature of children and the potential for training them, as well as the advent of powered printing presses, helps explain the surge in the number of guides for childrearing in the 1830s. Such books as Theodore Dwight's *The Father's Book* (1834), Dr. John Abbott's *The Mother at Home* (1833), Lydia Maria Child's *The Mother's Book* (1844), and Catherine Beecher's *Treatise on Domestic Economy* (1847) were the first wave of the literature on childcare that has been an integral part of American culture for one and a half centuries. Horace Bushnell's *Christian Nurture* was the most explicit rendering of the new view of the mother's responsibility for her children. Published in 1842, it was quickly withdrawn because of its criticism of conservative ministers, but by the 1860s, it had been reissued and was a "best-seller." Bushnell posited that a depraved state did not stem from an inherently evil nature, but from external sources, among them the failure to receive proper Christian training as a child. Like Horace Mann, he thought that there were separate stages of growth in an individual's lifetime—infancy, childhood, youth, and adulthood—and that childhood had its own special problems.

By the 1870s publications expressing a belief in innate depravity or infant damnation were rare. The prevailing new ideology was expressed in Jacob Abbott's *Gentle Measures in the Management and Training of Children* (1871). Jacob Abbott was the brother of John Abbott, author of *The Mother at Home,* and had himself written the enormously successful *Rollo* series of children's books. *Gentle Measures* went through several printings, and used the most contemporary scientific knowledge to explain children's behavior and to stress that "bad habits" were a result of improper training, not innate spiritual corruption. "Reason and affection," and "manoeuvre and artifice" were the tools for training a child; corporal punishment was a "last resort."[18]

Scientists joined the moral advisors in the literature on childcare of the late nineteenth century. Dr. L. Emmett Holt's *The Care and Feeding of Children* (1894), which remained in print for forty years after its initial publication, combined detailed explanations of nutritional needs with advice about the inevitable sicknesses and problems of childrearing. Holt was careful to point out that childcare meant more than food for the stomach; mothers were also responsible for the child's moral behavior and training. Such writers as Charlotte Perkins Gilman, whose *Concerning Children* was published in 1900, and William J. Shearer, whose *The Management and Training of Children* appeared in 1904, also emphasized "training" as the key to child development. They agreed with the Darwinians that heredity was a powerful agent in human destiny, but maintained that "influence" (nurture) was potent enough to counteract or overcome heredity. Gilman also believed that acquired characteristics were genetically transferable, a Lamarckian idea that conflicted with Darwinian biology.[19]

Physicians and such psychologists as G. Stanley Hall were enthusiastic and idealistic about children, but most of them had no experience of day-to-day childrearing. (Women writers were the obvious exceptions.) For mothers, the new ideology did not guarantee a well-behaved child, and they may have been less convinced than their advisors of inherent goodness. "Of all my babies I never have had one that began to so much trouble as this. He . . . has to be held most of the time he is awake. He roars around nights so that we cannot begin to get a good sleep," wrote Kate Huntington Taylor of Connecticut in 1876. Another mother, writing for *Heart and Home* in 1870, pointed out that it was her son who "taught" her that she "must screw [her] what-not to the wall, and wedge the books of [her] library, and sew down [her] tidies, and tie [her] vases, and put [her] phanthom bouquet on a high bracket, and . . . clear all frail beauty from [the] table and the bottom of the same what-not."[20]

If children were in one sense akin to angels, uncorrupted by the urban industrialism of America, then they presented their mothers with both a rare opportunity and an awesome responsibility. The middle-class home, in an ideological sense, became a kind of sanctuary. The persistence of the Gothic architectural and decorative style—trefoils, quatrefoils, and crockets—suggests this ecclesiastical or sanctuary ideal. Throughout the 1870s and 1880s, *Godey's* continued its practice of reproducing ideal building plans, most of which were in the Gothic style. The author of the housing column in the April 1879 issue of *The Household* lamented that "the square or bungalow form of dwelling . . . has grown unpopular of late years, more especially since Gothic has been the prevailing style."[21]

The home as a garden is an equally powerful idea in this period, again reflecting woman's role as nurturer. Indoor gardening in the bay windows that were popular from the middle nineteenth century onward was so commonplace that the women's magazines of the period usually printed articles about the care and treatment of plants. Women's responsibility for tending the realm of plants as well as children is emphasized by many of the pseudonyms of writers in women's magazines—Fanny Forrester, Fanny Fern, Grace Greenwood, Minni Myrtle, Lily Larkspur, and Jenny June.

The garden ideal of the home was a function of the conservative ideology of American history as a sort of "paradise lost."[22] Conservative critics found reason for alarm in the increasing numbers of Americans who lived in apartments and hotels, the beginning of women's entry into business, and the equal rights controversies of the last half of the nineteenth century. The importance attached to the mother's responsibility for nurturing children is in this context a rearguard action against urbanization and women's rights. Each child gave a mother a chance to start over, but each child also presented her with the possibility of failure: it was her responsibility if her children were not successful Christians in the capitalist "outer world."

One of the consequences of the new emphasis on nurturing was a nearly universal agreement among physicians that mothers ought to nurse their children. "Hand-raising," or feeding an infant some mixture other than human milk, was discouraged. In 1860 J. Stainback Wilson, a physician who regularly contributed a column to

Godey's, admonished mothers to resort "neither to hand-raising nor wet-nursing if they can possibly perform their maternal duties themselves." Women who refused to nurse when they were able to do so were characterized as "subservient to the requisitions of a spurious and unnatural civilization . . . misled by the seductive charms of the fashionable world." Such a mother was "guilty of a criminal injustice to her offspring," which, "in many cases, must result in the physical and moral destruction of her child." In 1889 *Good Housekeeping* warned that wet-nurses were to be avoided because they were "careless and indifferent," and might tend to quiet a disturbed infant "with a large dose of some stupefying drug while the mother partook of the unsubstantial pleasures of the ballroom." If a wet-nurse was, for some reason, a necessity, readers—predominantly white Anglo-Saxon Protestant women—were warned to protect future generations by closely examining the moral and physical character of the surrogate. "As to committing a child to any Irish women or freshly-imported foreigner, without the most rigid scrutiny . . . *never think of such a thing.*"[23]

In "Diet and Drinks of Nursing Women," Dr. Wilson advised mothers to concentrate on vegetables as their "principal diet," to refrain from "eating for two," and to avoid "highly seasoned dishes, rich gravies, fat port, salt bacon, pastries, acid and unripe fruits, pickles . . . coffee, wines, cordials, and various stimulating drinks, under the mistaken motion that they increase the milk and impart strength." "Drugging," especially with "opiates," was discouraged: "Mothers and nurses should use drugs very sparingly."[24] What all this advice means is that women were probably using drugs and opiates all the time. The cautions and prohibitions announce the gap between actual behavior and the ideology of medicine and health, or the expected role of women as nurturers. What was prohibited was probably closer to reality than the recommendation. The nursing bottle had been in existence since before 1800; nipples were introduced in 1835, and by 1885 more than one and one-half million bottles were sold annually (Fig. 18). This prompted Moses T. Runnells, in his 1886 essay "The Physical Degeneracy of American Women," to remark: "There can be no doubt whatever, that the true and essential function of these glands [breasts] at the present day is ornamental and aesthetic. Their noblest opportunities are not in the 'milky way,' but in the line of high art and realistic declination."[25]

Actual feeding practices evidently included feeding children solid foods when very young, including what Dr. J. N. Hanaford, *The Household*'s medical columnist, termed "the rind of fat pork." Dr. Charles P. Uhle, *Godey's* medical columnist, recommended donkey's milk, but allowed that "expense is very frequently a bar to its employment." He proposed sweetened cow's milk, rather than "all those preparations of arrow root, sago, tapioca, flour . . . crackers, bread, and sweetmeats." In the 1860s Wilson recommended a "sucking bottle," with a "roll of cloth" and "goose-quill" or "artificial nipple made of India rubber" for the women who did not nurse their children.

18. In spite of the admonitions of advisers, the nursing bottle industry was a booming one in the late nineteenth century. Pressed glass and tin bottles. English and American, 1865–1895.

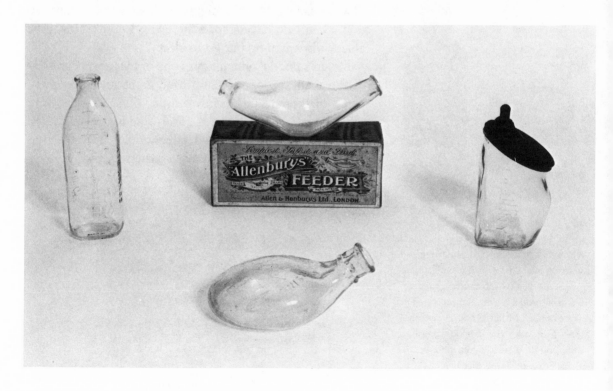

By 1889 bottle-feeding had become more sophisticated, showing the influence of Pasteur's work. An article in *Good Housekeeping* advised its readers to place bottles in an oven for a quarter of an hour, fill them with cow's milk, stopper them with cotton wool, and steam them for another thirty minutes to destroy "all germs." Nipples were to be boiled.[26]

Most physicians and advisors recommended weaning at the end of the child's first year. *Diet After Weaning,* a 1905 publication of the Mellin's Food Company of Boston, recommended weaning after one year, but not in hot weather or if the child was ill (Fig. 19). It suggested that the gradual separation of the infant from the breast include increasing amounts of Mellin's Food and cow's milk. If a child made weaning difficult, "the breast must be refused him entirely . . . hunger will soon compel him to take the artificial food. This is very trying to the mother, and if possible she should be out of sight and hearing until the ordeal is over." As Kate Huntington Taylor wrote in 1880: "I am weaning the baby nights, and dressmaking days, so that when I do have a spare moment, I don't seem to be able to do anything but go to sleep."[27]

Mellin's Food Company was one of the most aggressive of the many processed baby food companies that prospered in the late nineteenth century (Fig. 20). The firm utilized nearly every form of advertising in practice at the time. Canvassers distributed free samples door-to-door, stores displayed large colorful posters depicting ideal

19. The liquid-baby-food industry came of age in the latter decades of the nineteenth century when mechanized processing and production methods enabled manufacturers to produce inexpensive substitutes for mother's milk. Such products were extremely popular. Free sample, Mellin's Food. American, 1885. Murdock's Liquid Food. English, c. 1885. Bisque advertising figurine. W. H. Goss, Stoke-on-Trent, England, c. 1882.

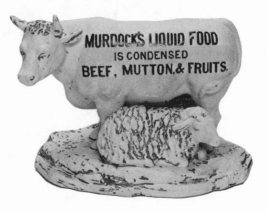

mothers and babies, and merchants gave away trade or advertising cards to consumers. The popular magazines of the day—*Godey's, Demorest's, The Household,* and *Good Housekeeping*—contained advertisements for the product. In addition, the magazines also carried letters to the editor testifying to the wonders of Mellin's. These were undoubtedly advertisements but, unlike today, were not (and did not have to be) identified as such.

The magazines were often the handmaidens of their advertisers, providing their readership with both a frightening specter and a means of salvation. In 1879 *The Household* ran a series of articles discussing "Food for Infants," in which the reality of a civilization in decline was presented:

> The statement is a startling and fearful one, that about one-half of the human race in civilized society die before the age of five years. This fact is all the more humiliating, since it is admitted that a similar mortality is not observed in savage life, leading us to infer that civilization is now adverse to the highest development of our physical being.[28]

The article linked this problem with a general ignorance of the nature of a healthy diet, criticizing especially the American tendency to load young children with starch. The authors concluded that mothers should use additives such as Mellin's Food because they were properly digestible and invigorating. In 1880 a "letter" appeared in the same magazine from a woman whose first four children died of "the American disease, dyspepsia," but her fifth was alive and thriving, thanks to her discovery of Mellin's Food. An advertisement for the product was run in the same issue.[29]

Mellin's also produced its own publications, and promised personal attention to all inquiries.

> If you are having trouble in feeding your baby. If his food disagrees with him, if he frets and cries, or loses

20. Advertisements such as this one for Mellin's Food helped engender a sense of trust in mothers. By offering both the product and the comforting advice, the corporation began to take the place of the doctor or family in an increasingly mobile and urban society. Advertising poster, Donaldson Brothers, Five Points, New York, c. 1890–1910.

weight, we wish you would write us, telling us fully just what the trouble is, how you are preparing the baby's food, and how you are feeding him. As soon as your letter reaches us we will send you a sample of Mellin's Food and will write you a personal letter telling you exactly how to use Mellin's Food for your baby.[30]

The corporation was taking on the role of advisor, competing with childcare writers, friends, relatives, and physicians. Mellin's offer also implies that there may have been a growing feeling of isolation, especially among young mothers. With fathers working away from home, and the servant population declining, the fears about child-rearing were magnified, especially because of the pressure and responsibility to raise healthy children (Fig. 21). As more and more research on infant and child physiology accumulated, the death of a child became less an act of God and more the mother's responsibility. Personal advice, even from a corporation, would have been welcome indeed as the extended family and support system of a more rural lifestyle was lost, and cities grew larger and more impersonal.

Stimulating the growth of strong, healthy children was not the only goal of the conscientious mother; diet had other implications for the nature of society. Many advocates of temperance located one root of American drinking in American eating habits, and therefore in women's failure to properly feed and train their children.

> It is one of women's rights to help cure intemperance in drinking by removing excitants from the food. By constantly stimulating, in early life, an unnatural appetite for condiments and dainties, the foundation of intemperance is often laid. Seasoning, therefore, should never be excessive.[31]

In spite of such warnings against "excitants," castor sets (matched bottles for condiments) were made and purchased in quantity, and the recipes in *Demorest's, Godey's,*

21. A healthy baby was a heavy baby. The emphasis placed on weight as a sign of health is evident in this sculptural group. "Weighing the Baby," painted cast plaster. John Rogers and Company, New York, 1876.

WEIGHING THE BABY

and *The Household* continued to call for such spices as cayenne and black pepper (Fig. 22). The surviving artifacts of dining suggest that no major change in American cooking or eating habits occurred, in spite of the demands of the extremely powerful temperance advocates.[32]

Old habits and traditions continued to be practiced in other realms of maternal responsibility. In spite of voluminous criticism in books and periodicals, mothers and nurses evidently continued the early-nineteenth-century practice of wrapping infants, sometimes rather tightly, in swaddling. In 1870 *The Bazar-Book of Decorum* chastised those who so clothed their offspring.

> The artificial process begins as soon as the child is born. The very swaddling-clothes are so many bonds by which it is restrained of the natural freedom of its body, and its growth so directed that it may assume a shape comfortable to some conventional notion or other. . . . Until the mother gets rid of the idea of *giving* a form to her child, and learns that it is her duty to accept what Nature bestows, the health and vigor of whole generations will continue to be sacrificed.[33]

The "artificial process" that began with birth proceeded from tight swaddling to, for some girls, a smaller version of the *bête noire* of dress-reformers, the corset. Abba Gould Woolson, one of the most ardent and vocal critics of women's dress, attacked "the absurdities and injuries of [children's] dress," especially the "weight and pressure of wide sashes, long full bows, and overskirts," comparing them to the "various excrescences with which adult spines are freighted." She favored the "unsullied, unrumpled, high-necked apron and ungarnished calico of former days," rather than the "miniature men and women" so clothed "by the dictates of the lastest fashion plate."[34]

In spite of dire warnings and good advice, the child's corset was a commonly used part of female children's dress, at least for public or formal occasions. The 1889 volume of *Good Housekeeping* carried a regular adver-

22. Castor sets were common accouterments of the Victorian American table. This inexpensive set would have held vinegar, oil, salt, pepper, and perhaps cayenne or some other spice. Cut glass and silver plate. Meriden Britannia Company, Meriden, Connecticut, 1886.

23. Inside front cover of *Good Housekeeping*, March 1, 1889.

tisement for the "Good Sense" corset waist, informing mothers that "your child must be kept healthy or she cannot be beautiful." It was guaranteed to "fit all ages, infants to adults," and was priced from fifty cents for the smallest size to two dollars for the "Ladies' " largest size (Fig. 23).[35] The advertisement reveals that the most important cultural concern for mother and daughter was physical appearance, part of the social ideology of display and presentation of status. Concern for the child's future appearance also prompted attacks on "leading strings." This apparatus was employed to help children learn to walk, but was thought to be "apt to cause the ugliest of deformities, the sinking of the neck between the shoulders."[36]

Attempts by parents to "beautify" their offspring with curled hair and jewelry also drew fire from domestic advisors. They criticized the practice of putting coral or gold necklaces and jewels on small children, as well as the custom of winding children's hair on "bobs" at night, in order to have curls by day. "They pay dearly for the glory of appearing in ringlets during the day," proclaimed *Miss Leslie's Behavior Book* in 1864, "if they are made to pass their nights lying upon a mass of hard, rough bobs."[37]

Here, then, was the mother's dilemma. She was attacked by reformers and advisors for her status-conscious practices of childrearing—for trying to "beautify" her children by bobbing their hair or dressing them to reflect the family's financial status or aspirations. Yet alongside the advice columns in women's magazines were powerful advertisements designed to encourage these very practices. The implication of these ads was that the mother was a failure if her children were not attractive. The sense of inadequacy for mothers, who were wrong whichever way they turned, must have been profound.

Bathing children in cold water, the standard procedure in ante-bellum America, was also under attack. "Nothing can be more absurd," wrote the editors of *Godey's* in 1870, "than the common practice of mothers and nurses washing children, no matter how sickly or unwell, with cold water, under the idea of bracing the constitution." They recommended "tepid bathing, temperance, and proper exercise" to make life "more agreeable and also prolonged."[38]

If children began fresh and free from evil, then it was important to commence their education at an early age. "Think, then, of their education as soon as they are born," advised the editors of *Godey's* in 1870. "The younger they are, the more tender and soft their minds, and the more susceptible to impressions." Since "there are more bad examples than good," if let alone, children's minds would be "nurtured in corruption." But six years later, the same magazine gave explicitly contrary advice: "There is far more mischief done in many families before the children reach the school-room than the best of governesses or tutors have power to eradicate. . . . The 'headaches' of early childhood are on the increase . . . children are over-excited in the nursery, and too early and too hard worked in the school-room; they are 'forced' as gardeners would say; for too early exhibition in the drawing-room."[39]

Education of the very young continued, however. By 1889 it took the form of the "kindergarten," which combined "manual training" with "organized play." "The eager, ardent kindergarten teacher . . . welcomes pupils in their third year if she can get them," but manual training, wrote the editors of *Good Housekeeping* in 1889, should begin at home.[40]

Idealized images of infant or youthful prodigies in the arts or other realms of learning were used to display the virtue and competence of the home environment. In a society in which display was everywhere—architecture, women's dress, and home furnishings—the "performance" was perhaps the ultimate presentation of middle-class power, influence, and achievement. The cultivation of children presented adults with a possible avenue to a world of unrealized fantasies and hopes which they might control. Just as on the issue of children's appearance and their physical condition, there were conflicts and contradictions within the advice women received and the social expectations they encountered on the subject of their children's intelligence and how to nurture it. Intelligent children—

24. With a diameter of only five inches, this chamber pot at first glance might be mistaken for a coffee cup. The rolled rim indicates its actual function. Earthenware with underglaze transfer print. Staffordshire, England, c. 1850–1880.

even prodigies—were a sign of intelligent, successful, "worthy" parents. Yet the pattern of advice for women was that they should never push their children when young. Social pressure evidently triumphed among the aspiring middle class, but at the price of guilt.

Throughout the nineteenth century, the ideology of childrearing was rooted in the idea that the family was "a little kingdom in miniature," as popular author Harvey Newcomb phrased it in 1851. "The father and mother are king and queen; and the children . . . are the subjects." Josiah Gilbert Holland urged parents to be certain that "every child born to you should learn among the first things it is capable of learning, that in your home your will is supreme, . . . keep all the time the reins of your authority steadily drawn." Catherine Beecher maintained that " '*Obey*, because your parent commands' was always a proper and sufficient reason. . . . Children can be very early taught, that their happiness . . . depends on the formation of habits of submission, self-denial, and benevolence." Newcomb instructed parents to "cultivate the love of useful labour," as his fellow author, editor, and publisher Timothy Shay Arthur put it, because "labour is not a curse, but a blessing; . . . to exert ourselves is something for which we have to be thankful." "Habits of industry" prevented idleness—a condition dreaded by good Protestants. "The idle brain," wrote a columnist for *The Household* in 1874, "is the devil's workshop. . . . Industry rightly understood and directed, calls into exercise benevolent feelings."[41]

One of the earliest types of instruction that most children experienced was toilet-training. The small size of children's chamber pots (Fig. 24) indicates the early age at which toilet-training was begun, and corresponds to the invocation in the November 1870 issue of *Godey's* that "children should be encouraged or . . . disciplined in performing for themselves every little office relative to their own toilet. . . . They should also keep their own clothes and other possessions in neat order." Thirty-five years later, only the apparatus had changed. In *Diet After Weaning*

(1905), Mellin's Food Company urged that mothers place children on a potty chair (rather than just the chamber pot) every night at 9 P.M., and at regular intervals during the day.[42]

As children grew from infants to "miniature adults," the social expectations for their behavior became more demanding, and consequently more a measure of a mother's competence. Manners—the public social behavior of children—were thus a topic of voluminous and intense concern for both advisory writers and parents. Deportment at the dining table, for example, occasioned numerous chapters, columns, and notes in the mass of childrearing manuals published in the late nineteenth century. Dining was one of the most formal rituals of the period. The dining room, like the parlor, was a space in which a family demonstrated—through manners, decoration, and fine china and silver—its wealth and station.

This display necessitated a well-trained child, and the ladies' magazines offered plenty of advice about how children ought to behave at the table. In the May 25, 1889 issue of *Good Housekeeping*, parents were urged to feed children under five years old before the adults sat for dinner, occasionally bringing them to the table for dessert. The child was to be assigned a seat "that shall be his or her place. A high chair is of course necessary for a child under four." The list of rules continued:

Teach it [the child] to take its seat quietly;
To use its napkin properly;
To wait patiently to be served;
To answer promptly;
To say thank you;
If asked to leave the table for a forgotten article or for any purpose to do so at once;
Never to interrupt and never to contradict;
Never to make remarks about the food . . . ;
Teach the child to keep his plate in order;
Not to handle the bread or to drop food on the cloth or floor;

To always say "Excuse me, please," to the mother when at home or to the lady or hostess when visiting, if leaving the table before the rest of the party;

To fold its napkin and to put back its chair or push it close to the table before leaving;

And after leaving the table not to return.

Good Housekeeping also suggested that a "special cup, plate, [and] spoon" be provided each child. "Lovely bread and milk sets, consisting of plate, bowl, and pitcher, can now be bought for two dollars. . . . Plates with the alphabet, or perhaps illustrating some fairy story, or maybe a geography lesson in the form of the map of the State in which the child lives, or some historical event pictured so as to tell a story" were part of the educational options open to parents (Fig. 25).[43]

Children's toys of the late nineteenth century—especially blocks, puzzles, maps, and card games—were also potential educators (Fig 26). Yet, unlike dining sets, they graphically demonstrate the gender-linked socialization process of the era. Toys for girls were directly tied to the roles which were open to them. Elementary education in

25. Children's plates were used to teach history, literature (as in *Robinson Crusoe*), the alphabet, or how to tell time. From left: English, c. 1880–1910; Brownhill's Pottery Company, Tunstall, England, 1887–1896; lithographed tin saucer, Bryan, Ohio, c. 1910.

26. "Sunday" toys, designed to teach the lessons of the Bible to young ones, allowed children to play on the Sabbath. Noah's Ark toy, carved wood, leather, and paper. American, c. 1900. Pilgrim's Progress board game, lithographed paper, cardboard, and wood. McLoughlin Brothers, New York, c. 1890. Toy church, lithographed paper, wood, and cardboard. R. Bliss Manufacturing Company, Pawtucket, Rhode Island, c. 1895.

decorating one's home could be learned from scrapbooks, in which girls could paste cut-out paper room settings (Fig. 27), and from dollhouses (Fig. 28), which by the late nineteenth century were becoming less expensive. Small-scale washing machines, carpet sweepers, stoves, and games directed girls toward housework imitative of their mothers (Fig. 29), and working miniature sewing machines helped "little women" sew clothes for their dolls (Fig. 30). The dolls themselves had changed. The little adults of the pre–Civil War era (Fig. 31) were gradually replaced by a new French form—the lifelike and idealized *Bébé*, or child-doll, who appeared to be about eight to twelve years old (Fig. 32). While both European and American doll makers still produced adultlike dolls, the French *Bébés* were the most popular and were quickly copied. Girls thus were directly engaged in mothering their own "children" and learning the role their culture anticipated for them.

THE CULT OF MOTHERHOOD

49

27. Child's scrapbook of cut-out room
interiors. Lithographs and engravings.
American, c. 1875.

28. R. Bliss was one of the most prominent
manufacturers of doll houses in the late
nineteenth century. Originally in the tool
business, Bliss adopted modern technology to
the production of his houses, which were
inexpensive enough to allow middle-class
parents to purchase them. Doll houses,
wood and lithographed paper.
R. Bliss Manufacturing Company,
Pawtucket, Rhode Island,
c. 1880–1900.

29. These miniatures of mother's tools, cast as playthings for little girls, were also for teaching them to be just like their most important role model, mother. Toy stove, cast iron and tin. American, c. 1910–1920. Child's washer, wood and tin. American, 1850–1900. Toy carpet sweeper, wood, wire, and steel. Bissell Manufacturing Company, Portland, Maine, c. 1900.

Boys were granted a wider spectrum of acceptable play activities. The toys of male youth do not indicate the sort of direct occupational correlation found in those of their female counterparts. Fire engines, trains, and pistols are more suggestive of a generalized attitude toward the world than encouragement for a particular career choice (Fig. 33). These toys emphasize movement, and to some extent control, over the landscape, just as women's toys were part of the domestic sphere of staying in one place. Toy soldiers may have been more intimately linked to a desirable career (probably as an officer), but most of the professional occupations to which the middle-class male aspired were not translated into toys. This may have been because the paraphernalia of those jobs (physicians excepted) was not especially conducive to play (how could a toy manufacturer translate a lawyer's equipment into a toy?). Or perhaps it was because of some cultural need to maintain distance between middle-class adult male activities and those of children. This suggests a cultural equation of women and children. Both were dependent on men.

Women with one child were considered negligent be-

30. These sewing machines are working models of the larger ones used by adult women. They enabled girls to sew doll clothes, and develop the sewing skills they would need in the future. Left: painted cast iron and sheet metal. J. G. Folsom, Winchenden, Massachusetts, c. 1864. Right: painted cast iron, steel, and nickel. Foley and Williams Manufacturing Company, Chicago, c. 1900.

31. Dolls of the early and mid-nineteenth century resembled little women rather than children or infants. Doll with papier-mâché head and cloth body. Ludwig Grenier and Company, Philadelphia, c. 1858–1862.

cause they were denying their national duty to bear and rear healthy, middle-class (WASP) children to counteract the influx of immigrants. Moreover, siblings were supposed to bring forth feelings of self-denial and benevolence in each other. As *The Household* phrased it in 1874, "Unfortunate is that mother who has but one child to train for her country and her God, unfortunate, indeed, is that child who has no brothers and sisters to call forth his generous sympathies and self-denying actions." But siblings were often contentious, and tested the power and influence of mothers as the primary agents of socialization. Younger children, wrote Catherine Beecher, "assume airs of equality; and if allowed to treat one class of superiors in age and character disrespectfully . . . will soon use the privilege universally. . . . [They] are most apt to be pert, forward, and unmannerly." The expectations and theories of children's nature—benevolent and good—contrasted with the belligerence and antisocial behavior of children. The explanation for this set of apparent contradictions turned upon the familiar role of women as controllers of the domestic scene. The responsibility for maintaining domestic order rested with women; the house was the "woman's kingdom and . . . should be the place for the practice of all the little courtesies of refined life; parents with children, and children with each other."[44]

As children grew into adulthood, maternal responsibility broadened and the patterns and rhythms of their training changed. For boys, home was where they could return for support and comfort after launching into the wider world of school, sports, politics, labor, and industry. Their training as social beings came increasingly from outside the home. For middle-class girls, home and family were the entire world and always would be. Their social, moral, sexual, and domestic education was the sole responsibility of their mother. H. Maria George asserted in *The Household* that "each mother must see to it that the most important branch of her daughters' education is not neglected in their youth. The time is past when it was considered fashionable for a young lady to be unskilled in domestic duties." To be a "well-trained woman" was to be "courteous, cheerful, polite, pious, moral and benevolent" and to avoid "gossip, slander, tale-telling, fault-finding, grumbling, and public display of family quarrels." The model young woman was not stubborn or self-centered, had good table manners, showed respect for her parents, and was "industrious and good-natured."[45] With these qualities, a young woman would be able to obtain her culturally determined goal of marriage and motherhood. Decorum became the middle-class dowry.

In addition to the advice a mother could read to help her raise her children, there was, by the 1850s, a body of literature she could direct her daughter to read. "Let her read in peace," urged *Miss Leslie's Behavior Book*. "It will do her more good than anything else, and lay the foundation of an intelligent mind."[46]

Imaginative literature for children and young adults began to emerge as a popular literary form in the 1830s, as ideas of youthful goodness took hold. By 1856, Peck and Bliss of Philadelphia offered three sets of these books: two

32. Childlike dolls were designed to allow girls to play at being mother. Children themselves were becoming increasingly important, as the American attitude toward them changed. Left: doll with bisque head, composition body. Right: doll with bisque lower arms, hands, and head, kid body. Emile Jumeau, Paris, France, 1875–1885.

33. Boy's toy locomotive, "The 999," cast iron. American, c. 1910.

of twelve and one of sixteen volumes. Many of these were behavior instruction manuals, more direct and heavy-handed than such fanciful yet moralistic works as *The Swiss Family Robinson* (1812–13) and *Andersen's Fairy Tales* (1835–42).

The most popular fictional hero of the pre–Civil War era was probably that nine-year-old paragon of goodness, Rollo. Created by Jacob Abbott, Rollo epitomized the principled and pious scion of virtue delineated in such youth advisory books as Henry Ward Beecher's *Lectures to Young Men* (1845) and J. M. Austin's *Golden Steps for Youth of Both Sexes* (1852). Rollo was the consummate Christian. Whatever he did, wherever he went, whenever he was tempted, Rollo behaved as a minister would want him to. He protected women, and emerged triumphant from his many encounters with unscrupulous and unprincipled evil-doers. Rollo was good, in a world where goodness was always rewarded in the end. The world's challenges were difficult (Rollo was *On the Atlantic* in 1858 and *In Europe* for a series of books thereafter), but never so testing as to cause Rollo to question or change the principles he learned at home.[47]

Abbott's parallel writer in the post–Civil War era was Horatio Alger, Jr. Each of the Alger books had the same basic formula: a young lad, who is not always perfect, works diligently, and gets lucky. If Rollo was a paragon of piety, Dick and Harry Walton and Alger's other young men were products of a more secular heroic mold—rugged, manly, and full of "pluck." The other critical difference was that Rollo was a model youth who embodied the contemporary requisites of obedience and subservience to adults. Many of Alger's heroes were somehow superior to his adult characters; they were able to save their elders, not in the proto-Christian spiritual way of a dying Little Eva in *Uncle Tom's Cabin* (1852), but by making enough money to save the old homestead.[48]

The notion that children could save good, but powerless, adults, or defeat evil ones, was celebrated in the burst of imaginative children's literature published after 1885. *The*

Brownies, Their Book appeared in 1887, and these little people with magical powers were so successful that they became an iconographic idiom for American children. Brownie books, dolls, and games proliferated (Fig. 34), and their success was in part attributable to their magic powers, which allowed them to mischievously taunt evil adults (which appealed to children), while maintaining an essentially moral world order (which appealed to adults).[49]

The young heroes, heroines, and anthropomorphic animal characters of late-nineteenth-century children's novels contended with an outside world that was becoming increasingly hostile. Beatrix Potter's *Peter Rabbit* (1904) barely escaped death in the cabbage patch. Home was heaven for the rabbits, as it was for *Black Beauty* (1897) and Jim Hawkins of *Treasure Island* (1892). Home and its guardian, mother, were the counterpoints to the urban industrial world.

34. Palmer Cox created an enormously successful world for children. "Brownie" books, toys, and tableware were part of a complex miniature world in which good little people triumphed over bad (usually adult) characters. Porcelain match holder, German or American, c. 1900. Porcelain plate, German, c. 1890. *The Brownies, Their Book*, New York, 1890. "Brownie" toy, American, c. 1900.

The key to this view of the home was in the ideological vision of motherhood. A famous engraving from the 1860 volume of *Godey's,* "The Light of Home," illustrates the point (see frontispiece). A mother sits with one child on her lap and two others playing at her feet. The editors explain the significance of the image: "The perfection of womanhood . . . is the wife and mother, the center of the family, the magnet that draws man to the domestic altar, that makes him a civilized being, a social Christian. The wife is truly the light of the home." Thirteen years later, in the same magazine, Thomas Gentry portrayed the mother as "a being around whom clusters all that is eminently good and truly grand," and urged the young woman to "listen to the sound teachings" of her mother to "occupy that station in life which your Creator has designed you for, where characters are moulded which shall sway sceptres or shape the destinies of worlds." Father is nowhere in the image.[50]

As the body of knowledge about human origins increased in the nineteenth century, the concept of home as sanctuary and garden and the conviction that children were born innocent merged with theories of anthropology and evolutionary biology to strengthen the conviction that matriarchy was the basis for the good Christian community. Elizabeth Cady Stanton summarized this position in 1891: "Careful historians now show that the greatest civilizing power all along the pathway of natural development has been found in the wisdom and tender sentiments growing out of motherhood. For the protection of herself and her children women made the first home in the caves of the earth; then huts with trees in the sunshine." Stanton maintained that "clearly the birth of civilization must be sought in the attempt of women at self-preservation during the period of pregnancy and lactation."[51] This view coexisted with the more aggressive vision of the followers of social Darwinist Herbert Spencer, who maintained that those same sentiments of motherhood—piety and love of the helpless—were the characteristics that restricted women to the home for their own survival.

Science, religion, and the political structure of late-nineteenth-century America formed a powerful force for inequality between men and women. There are two basic responses to situations of persistent inequality: the dominated sector can actively or passively resist, generally at great risk to itself; or the dominated sector can build elaborate intellectual rationales for its position, and claim some future reward of a generally nonmaterial nature. Tennessee Claflin, Victoria Woodhull, Amelia Bloomer, Susan B. Anthony, Elizabeth Cady Stanton, and others actively resisted the secondary status of women in the late nineteenth century, but the vast majority of middle-class women accepted their position.

Writers like Josiah Gilbert Holland assured them that "Heaven . . . has given special favors to your sex, through this simple fact or principle of dependence. It is your work to soften and refine men. Men living without you, by themselves, become savage and sinful. The purer you are, the more are they restrained, and the more are they elevated." To avoid being a "pet and plaything," women had "the poor and the sick to visit; . . . a family to rear and train."[52]

Political and social power properly belonged to women only as maternal responsibility.

> Their husbands are to them only children of a larger growth, to be loved and cared for very much in the same way as their real children. It is the motherly element which is the hope, and is to be the salvation of the world. The higher a woman rises in moral and intellectual culture, the more is the sensual refined away from her nature, and the more pure and perfect and predominating becomes her motherhood. The real woman regards all men, be they older or younger than herself, not as possible lovers, but as sort of step-sons towards whom her heart goes out in motherly tenderness.[53]

Motherhood was simultaneously endowed with enormous responsibility and limited authority. Women were supposed to effect changes in the rottenness around them by indirect means—by "influence"—yet at the same time they were not supposed to be able to comprehend that society, either because they were too frail, too burdened with the chores of childcare, or intellectually inferior. American men and women may have rued the "deterioration" of American society from colonial days, but male activity and female support affirmed their society's new commitment to economic expansion, urbanization, and technological innovation. Sadness over the lost Golden Age was used to manipulate women, but was never allowed to interfere with commercial enterprise. By valuing precisely those qualitites of sentiment and community which social and economic reality denied or ignored, the cult of motherhood became an institutionalized, but powerless, conscience for capitalism.

There is much said and written now-a-days about "What shall we teach the girls?" Teach them to be neat, orderly in their habits, and to work, of course. . . . In many cases, mothers will let girls do certain things about housework, while they themselves perform the more difficult tasks. . . . When [daughters] are married and the whole round of duties falls upon their shoulders, they find it hard to rightly perform those same labors.[1]

THREE

CLEANLINESS and GODLINESS

THE
TYRANNY
OF
HOUSEWORK

Housework, the creation and maintenance of the domestic environment, was both an extension of a woman's role in nurturing the family and a vehicle for it. A clean and pleasant home created a place for the inculcation of proper middle-class values; it also set a standard for a woman's daughters to emulate and her sons to expect in their own adulthood. Total devotion of a woman to her husband required that she be an exemplary steward of his home. As Shirley Murphy stipulated in *Our Homes and How to Make Them Healthy* (1883): "A clean, fresh, and well-ordered house exercises over its inmates a moral, no less than physical influence, and has a direct tendency to make members of the family sober, peaceable, and considerate of the feelings and happiness of each other."[2]

A woman was measured by the state of her home. It was the prevailing orthodoxy that if the yard and garden were untended, the house unpainted, and the rooms neglected and unkempt, the family would be less moral and less successful than one residing in a carefully maintained home. One domestic advisor warned:

There are numerous instances of worthy merchants and mechanics whose efforts are paralyzed, and their hopes chilled by the total failure of the wife in her sphere of duty; and who seek solace under their disappointment in the wine-party, or the late convivial supper. Many a day-laborer, on his return at evening from his hard toil is repelled by the sight of a disorderly house and a comfortless supper . . . and he makes his escape to the grog-shop or the underground gambling room.[3]

In the late nineteenth century, housekeeping meant cooking, cleaning, doing laundry, and sewing. Cooking was the clearest extension of the mother's nurturing role, and therefore a "department of the highest importance which belongs wholly to a woman's province. . . . If we are to be a vigorous and enduring race, we must have both well-selected food and good cookery."[4] Daily cooking was seldom recorded in the diaries and journals kept by nineteenth-century women, probably because it was so commonplace. Recipes and menus in popular women's magazines suggest that women were expected to prepare what by twentieth-century terms were elaborate meals— beginning with a large breakfast, which typically consisted of bread, cooked potatoes, cooked or raw fruit, and beef, ham, or fish. (In cities and towns, large breakfasts meant that women had to rise earlier, and perhaps retire later than other family members. On farms, of course, men rose at least as early to complete the pre-breakfast chores of feeding and milking livestock.)

In addition to the daily routine of meal preparation, nearly all women baked on Tuesdays or Thursdays and Saturdays.[5] Baking was regarded as a separate task, and even those women who had a domestic servant usually did their own baking—an important measure of their domestic skill (Fig. 35). Almira MacDonald, the mother of three children and the wife of an attorney in Rochester, New York, baked nearly every Saturday.

> Saturday, April 19, 1856: Baked as usual today.
> Saturday, July 7, 1870: Baked this morning & c. Am feeling miserable.
> Saturday, March 30, 1878: very ill . . . made lemon pies & c.
> Saturday, August 15, 1885: baked today.
> Saturday, August 22, 1885: baked.
> Saturday, August 29, 1885: baked bread, cake today.
> Saturday, September 5, 1885: baked bread, cakes.[6]

In 1850 less than ten percent of the bread consumed in the United States was commercially baked. By 1900 the figure had risen to twenty-five percent, but baking was still done at home by the vast majority of the population.[7]

Baking bread by the two most common methods took nearly twenty-four hours. On the evening before a baking day, the sponge for white bread—a combination of yeast, sugar, water, and flour—was set and left to rise throughout the night. The following morning, the sponge was formed into loaves and left to rise again while the "brown bread" and "ornamental" cakes and pastries were made. Dried fruits to be used as pie filling were also prepared the night before. The alternative method began the morning before the baking day. Yeast and sugar were added to water, and left to ferment until noon. Then flour was added to produce a batter, which was left to rise through the afternoon. After the evening meal, more flour and shortening (generally lard) were mixed into the yeast mixture to form a smooth dough, which was then left to rise overnight. The following morning the dough was shaped into loaves, set aside to rise for another forty-five minutes, and baked.[8]

Nineteenth-century kitchen ranges were fueled by coal or wood. Though most of them were more reliable than the open hearth and beehive oven arrangements of the eighteenth and early nineteenth century, they were nonetheless difficult to master. Considerable practice and a knowledge of the intensity with which different woods burned were required in order to get successful results from the baking process. Still, ovens like the Sterling Range, billed as the "Perfect Baking and Roasting Oven," were appreciated (Fig. 36). Susan Huntington Hooker, whose husband worked at her parents' nursery in Rochester, New York, wrote her sister in 1886: "We are again living in our house and find our improvements far ahead of my most sanguine expectations. Our hot and cold water and new magic range make the work so much easier that when we are settled it seems as though we had saved one-half of our work."[9] These cast-iron stoves were located in the kitchen, near the central chimney, into which they were vented (Fig. 37). Often they were accompanied by tall, cylindrical hot-water heaters, which left their traces as

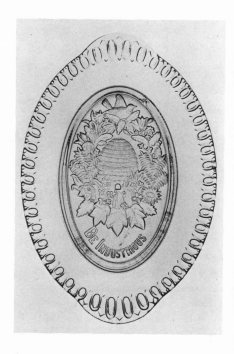

35. Even on an item as common as this bread tray the message is clear: work is a virtue. Pressed glass. Iowa City Manufacturing Company, Iowa, c. 1880.

burned scars in kitchen floors of the later nineteenth century. The hot-water heater was immensely popular because it eliminated the tedium and peril of boiling large quantities of water for use in laundry and kitchen tasks.

Cooking and baking were only a part of the food production in most households. Almira MacDonald's fruit preservation in 1870 was typical of the period:

> June 20: I have a stiff neck and shoulder but have made ten pounds of strawberry jam.
>
> July 6: I made ten quarts of black raspberries into jam today.
>
> July 7: I made ten quarts of black raspberry jam, four pounds of currant jelly.
>
> July 8: I canned five quarts of berries.
>
> July 12: Made three and one-half quarts red raspberries and currants.

36. The Sterling range was widely advertised in the late nineteenth century as the perfect baking and roasting oven. Advertisement in *Jury Magazine*, November 2, 1889.

July 13: Ten quarts raspberries, two quarts currant juice, two jars cherries; pickled some.

August 25: I canned fourteen pounds plums this morning.

September 28: I canned three-fourths bushel peaches (twelve jars).

September 29: Finished the bushel of peaches.

October 14: Canned one bushel of quinces.

October 15: Busy at quince Marmalade, and moving fruit to other cubboards [*sic*].[10]

In 1879 MacDonald pickled raspberries and cucumbers, and made catsup, while canning approximately the same volume of fruit. In 1885 she increased her production of all preserves, especially raspberries. She canned twenty-two pounds of them.

Cherry-stoners, crank-driven machines that sliced the fruit and discharged the pits into a separate container (Fig. 38), eased canning cherries, but scalding and peeling peaches or apricots, hulling strawberries and raspberries,

38. Cherry pitters made preserving easier at the turn of the century. Cast iron and painted wood. New Standard Corporation, Mount Joy, Pennsylvania, c. 1875–1900.

and washing currants still demanded tedious labor. In 1874 a fruit, wine, or jelly press cost three dollars but, for most women, jelly-making entailed the method described in an 1889 issue of *Good Housekeeping*:

Rinse [currants] in cold water . . . and drain in a colander. Then remove stems and leaves and put the currants in a porcelain or granite ware kettle and place in hot oven to scald. When the fruit is well broken strain all through a bag, squeezing hard to get all the juice. Strain a second time through a clean bag and then measure, allowing one pound of granulated sugar to one pint of juice. Put juice and sugar back into the kettle, and place over the fire and stir every moment till the sugar is dissolved. . . . When the juice is scalding hot pour into the glasses, previously made *hot* in water. Fill the glasses quite full and let stand a day or two. Then sift powdered sugar over the tops or put on white paper dipped in brandy. Cover with tin covers or paste up with paper and label.[11]

Canning fruit enabled women to vary "the winter regime of stewed and baked apples, prunes and cranberry sauce,"

39. Some fruit spoons had depictions of the fruit to be consumed on the handle or the bowl. Others, like these, have designs from nature. Silver fruit spoons. American, c. 1880.

but promised the canner "a hot stifling kitchen . . . stained hands and [an] aching back" (Fig 39).[12]

Neither the drudgery of home canning, nor the availability of commercially processed fruits and vegetables by the 1880s, discouraged the practice in the increasingly urban Northeast (Fig. 40). Many late-nineteenth-century town and city dwellers, having grown up on farms, considered home canning a tradition and responsibility.

> Canned fruit and vegetables have become one of the staple articles of food in our country as well as a leading article of export to other lands. Such goods may be bought of any respectable grocer and form usually a large part of their stock in trade. Still many people have a prejudice in favor of home canned goods.

> She never dreamed of giving up entirely and using tin-canned fruit from the grocery! That was never as fresh and nice, was more expensive, and besides too often tasted "tinny."[13]

Drying fruit, especially apples, was a traditional and widely practiced method of food preservation. Throughout the

40. Nearly all types of foodstuffs—fruits, vegetables, and meats—were available in cans by the end of the nineteenth century. Directions for serving meats indicated that the consumer was to boil the sealed can for approximately twenty minutes before serving. This practice probably prevented some disease, but also produced a tinny taste. Processed-food labels for tin cans. Forbes Lithograph Company, Boston, c. 1880.

41. Clamped to a work surface, the apple parer removed the skin of the fruit by means of a blade that was held against the apple while the fruit turned. Cast iron. American, c. 1880.

Northeast, sliced apples were placed on racks, to be dried either by the sun or the heat of a stove. The wide variety of apple parers and corers marketed in the late nineteenth century—more than eighty patents were issued between 1803 and 1874—attests to the importance of the fruit as a staple of American cooking (Fig. 41).[14]

Urban as well as rural families often raised livestock. The Huntington family, owners of a seed business and nursery in Rochester, New York, kept swine on their grounds, enduring both the extra labor and the disruption of weekly routine caused by the preparation of slaughtered animals for storage. In December 1867 Alcesta Huntington wrote to her mother:

Norah trying out lard, cleaning pig's feet and heads. Tomorrow I suppose we shall make head cheese. The sausages are to be made and put into skins uptown. . . . Now to explain why we were washing at eleven o'clock at night. Yesterday Horace had made arrangements for killing the pigs, but they would need the stove of course so our washing was to wait, but after dinner, Terrie, [thought] it a pity to lose such a good fire, and so much hot water as was left.[15]

The men of the family arranged for or did the actual slaughtering of most large stock, although women often killed and dressed poultry and did all the rest.

Instructions for preparing a slaughtered animal for storage appeared in cookbooks, housekeeping manuals, and periodicals. The February 1879 issue of *The Household* instructed readers to wash the butchered pig's head and place it in brine under a weight. The feet were "boiled until the bones would drop out"; the meat minced and packed in a crock. Salt was rubbed into the heart and tongue, which were stored for two days and boiled. The liver was boiled and chopped, combined with corn or some other grain, cooled, and packed in crocks. The ham and shoulder were salted, and the remaining bones were boiled to make broth.[16]

In the 1870s butchering tasks were performed with vessels made of steel, tin, copper, or cast-iron; some were procelain-coated. By the last quarter of the nineteenth century, many of these articles in the middle-class kitchen had been replaced by a popular innovation—"granite ware" (Fig. 42). The name refers to the mottled gray appearance of a porcelain-like coating applied to sheet iron or steel. The advantages of this material were lightness and durability. By 1880, "Almost any kitchen utensil that a housekeeper needs she can now get of this ware. Coffee pots, tea pots, syrup cups, water pails of all sizes from two cups up, tea kettles, dinner pots, kettles of all sizes from half to several gallons, saucepans with tight-fitting lids and long handles, all sizes, pie dishes, dish pans, spiders or frying pans, and long iron spoons for cooking purposes."[17] Aluminum utensils were just beginning to be introduced in 1910.

Most kitchens had a variety of mills or grinders for pulverizing dry goods and condiments. The most common pepper and spice mills were cylindrical, with a small crank on top, and could be obtained for twenty to thirty cents

42. Mail-order catalogs of the late nineteenth century are full of advertisements for graniteware utensils. Because of their low price, unbreakability, light weight, and easily cleaned surfaces, they were immensely popular from the moment they were produced. Agateware colander, preserving pot, and mixing bowl, enameled sheet metal and iron. American, 1860–1910.

43. Canned preground coffee was not available to most consumers until the turn of the century, but whole beans were inexpensive, and there was a wide variety of coffee grinders available. Left: cast iron. Esten Valor Manufacturing Company, Philadelphia, c. 1870. Center: wood, cast iron, earthenware, glass, and pewter. American, c. 1910. Right: painted steel. Landers, Frary and Clark Company, New Britain, Connecticut, c. 1905.

from such mass-marketing firms as Sears Roebuck and Company. Coffee mills operated on the same principle, and could be obtained in three basic forms. The least expensive variety (priced from eighteen to forty-eight cents in the Sears Roebuck catalog of 1902) consisted of a crank atop a wooden box with a small drawer to remove ground coffee. A second alternative was wall-mounted, and consisted of a jar or tin which dispensed whole beans into a crank-driven grinder. The ground beans fell into a removable container below the grinder. The least expensive of the four mills of this type offered by Sears Roebuck was twenty-nine cents; the deluxe model was seventy-three cents, and boasted both a glass hopper (for the beans) and receiver. The most elaborate coffee mills were the double-sided flywheel types, which were most commonly used in commercial establishments. The smallest mill of this style cost two dollars and forty cents, and was capable of grinding one-quarter pound of coffee per minute. The most expensive variety (twenty-seven dollars) was a floor model which weighed more than three hundred pounds, stood over six and one-half feet tall, and was intended for use in "high class grocery and coffee stores" (Fig. 43).[18] Coffee mills were necessities because coffee was an integral part of breakfast and lunch, and became increasingly popular as an after-dinner custom in the late nineteenth century.

Chopping and mincing meat were made less laborious after the Civil War by the mass production and distribution of the hand-crank meat grinder (Fig. 44). Yet advertisements for chopping and mincing knives—broad blades with curved bottoms and handles connected to the top—indicate that the meat grinders and slicers performed some but not all of those chores. These knives were generally used with large semispherical wooden bowls or oblong trays in which the material to be chopped or minced was placed (Fig. 45).

Almost all kitchens had butter-making apparatuses. Churns were of two basic types: the "dash" or up-and-down plunger churn, and the circular crank churn, popular after 1870. Butter spades, wooden triangular-shaped paddles, were used in a churn to make butter or to form the

44. The hand meat-grinder—whose form has remained unchanged for at least a century—was an essential tool in late-nineteenth-century American cookery. Many recipes published in mass-market periodicals called for minced or chopped meats, and this machine made those jobs much easier. Meat, nut, and bread grinder, cast iron and wood. Landers, Frary, and Clark Company, New Britain, Connecticut, c. 1897–1910.

45. Despite the advent of the meat grinder, the bowl and chopping knives were still common tools for chopping and mincing. Chopping bowl, burled maple. American, c. 1850–1900. Mincing knives, cast steel and wood. American, 1870–1890.

finished product into bricks (Fig. 46). Wooden molds and butter "hands" (grooved paddles) were used to form butter into fancy shapes.

Advice was abundant for the woman seeking help in the arrangement and management of the kitchen. In her popular manual *From Attic to Cellar* (1892), Elizabeth F. Holt argued that the ideal kitchen "ought to be planned for first. Young people about to marry usually commence with the parlour and end up with the kitchen. . . . This is a mistake they soon discover themselves." Holt maintained that two wooden tables were necessary, one for food service and one for food preparation, and she recommended that the latter be covered with an "enamelled [oil] cloth." A chest of drawers to store table linens and a fold-up ironing table, as well as the obligatory stove, hot-water heater, and icebox were advised. "A woman's workshop ought to be as well supplied with working tools as her husband's is." "Three strong wooden chairs, and one comfortable wooden rocking chair should be included

46. Some of the indispensable tools for an American kitchen in the late nineteenth century. Top row: rolling pins, wood and porcelain. American. Bottom row, from left: meat pounder, potato masher, strainer, whisk, and pie crust jaggers, porcelain and wood. American, c. 1885. Far right: two pie crust jaggers, carved ivory and abalone shell. American, 1850–1900.

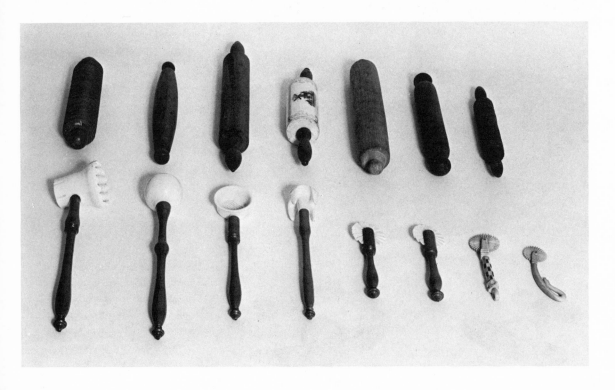

in the kitchen furniture," and the kitchen should be "provided with a hardwood floor which can be easily washed and kept clean."[19]

Many storage and work surface requirements were met by an invention of the late nineteenth century, the "Hoosier" cabinet, which combined a sliding zinc-covered or porcelain tabletop with cupboard space, sugar and flour bins (sometimes with built-in flour sifters), a tin-lined breadbox, and sliding storage shelves (Fig. 47). Generally made of oak, the "Hoosier"—the brand name became

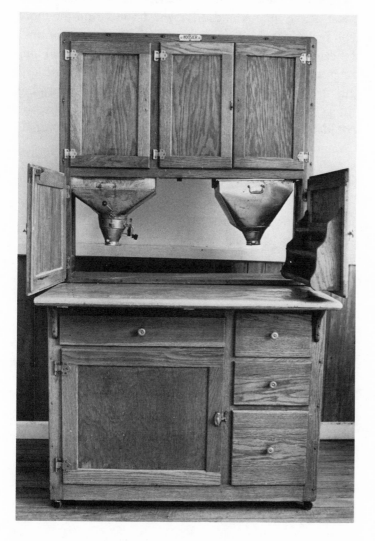

47. A "Hoosier" cabinet opened to show its functional storage areas. The chute on the left side is for flour and has a sifter built into the bottom. The chute on the right side is for sugar. The flat, unadorned surfaces are designed for easy cleaning. Oak plywood and sheet zinc. Hoosier Manufacturing Company, Indianapolis, Indiana, c. 1910.

generic—helped to answer the cooking needs of both the smaller, apartment-size kitchens of the city, and the full-size kitchens in which the cook desired greater efficiency.

Efficiency was the ideal, but certainly not the norm, regardless of a family's financial station. The Huntingtons' nursery business was profitable enough to allow the parents to spend each winter in the 1870s and 1880s with their son in Mandarin, Florida. Left to run their parents' house and business, daughters Alcesta and Susan struggled in the kitchen. Alcesta wrote: "I have been very busy in the kitchen most of the day. The state the kitchen is in most of the time would drive you frantic. And the more you try to put things in order the greater the confusion." Fifteen years later, in 1883, little had changed in the Huntington household: "We have a young and inexperienced girl in our kitchen and all my time is given to helping things move there." For those with no "help," the kitchen could be enslaving. Harriet Bailie wrote in her journal: "Mama, with all her noble and ennobling ambitions, is a slave to the kitchen, making something out of nothing, day after day. . . . Always haunting us is debt."[20]

Women sent out their washing and ironing or consigned it to domestic help whenever possible. These chores, which were extremely taxing, were one avenue of economic survival for women, usually married, who were unable to secure other forms of employment. Laundering and ironing the clothing of the middle-class family seems to have been a biweekly operation. A family's load of washing commanded a wage of two to two and one-half dollars throughout the period.[21]

For those unable to hire the laundry out to a laundress, Monday was the most common laundry day. M. H. Cornelius, in *The Young Housekeeper's Friend* (1868), described a method for laundering clothes that was unchanged by the turn of the century. She advised women to sort the laundry, so as to wash delicate and white fabrics first, calicos and ginghams second, and woolens last. The process required two large washtubs: the first to be filled with very warm soapy water, the second to be used for rinsing. She recommended rubbing all materials in the soapy water, but urged women to forego use of a washboard for delicate fabrics. All other clothing was then to be scrubbed on the board or agitated with a plunger. The wet clothes were to be laid out in the second tub, which was empty. Hot water was then dipped from a vat, heating on the stove (or filled from the water heater), and poured over the clothes. Next, the tub was covered, soap added, and the clothes boiled for thirty minutes. After being drained in a basket, the clothes were returned to the tub, rinsed with clean water and bluing, wrung out by hand or with a wringer, and hung to dry, either outside or on a drying rack. (Fig. 48).[22]

"We can never, under the most favorable circumstances, get up any enthusiasm, over a washing day," wrote Barbara Brandt in *The Household*. The "weekly affliction," as she termed it, was so universally abhorrent that magazines throughout the late nineteenth and early twentieth centuries offered hints on how to ease the burden. Eliminating ruffles and dressing less in white and more in printed cottons were recommended by *The Household*, as was a large supply "of undergarments—separate ones for the day and night, so that these may be changed as often

48. Requisites for the laundry room. From left: copper and wood wash boiler, Revere Copper Company, American, c. 1910; copper and tin wash plunger, American, c. 1880–1885; cast-iron, wood, and rubber wringer, Lovell Manufacturing Company, Erie, Pennsylvania, c. 1898. Foreground: wood, steel, and cast-iron drying rack, L. Hopkins Company, Niles Grove, Pennsylvania, c. 1887.

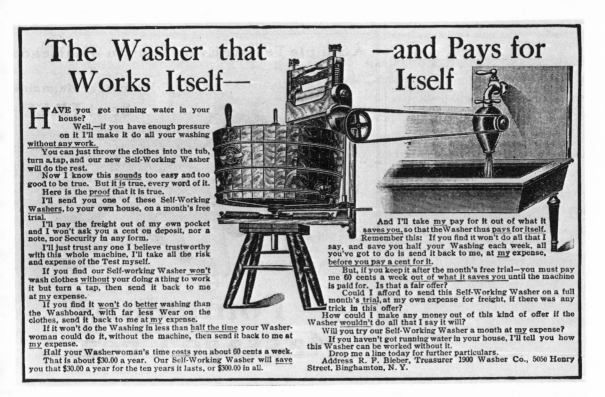

The Washer that Works Itself— —and Pays for Itself

HAVE you got running water in your house?
Well,—if you have enough pressure on it I'll make it do all your washing without any work.
You can just throw the clothes into the tub, turn a tap, and our new Self-Working Washer will do the rest.
Now I know this sounds too easy and too good to be true. But it is true, every word of it. Here is the proof that it is true.
I'll send you one of these Self-Working Washers, to your own house, on a month's free trial.
I'll pay the freight out of my own pocket and I won't ask you a cent on deposit, nor a note, nor Security in any form.
I'll just trust any one I believe trustworthy with this whole machine, I'll take all the risk and expense of the Test myself.
If you find our Self-working Washer won't wash clothes without your doing a thing to work it but turn a tap, then send it back to me at my expense.
If you find it won't do better washing than the Washboard, with far less Wear on the clothes, send it back to me at my expense.
If it won't do the Washing in less than half the time your Washerwoman could do it, without the machine, then send it back to me at my expense.
Half your Washerwoman's time costs you about 60 cents a week.
That is about $30.00 a year. Our Self-Working Washer will save you that $30.00 a year for the ten years it lasts, or $300.00 in all.

And I'll take my pay for it out of what it saves you, so that the Washer thus pays for itself.
Remember this: If you find it won't do all that I say, and save you half your Washing each week, all you've got to do is send it back to me, at my expense, before you pay a cent for it.
But, if you keep it after the month's free trial—you must pay me 60 cents a week out of what it saves you until the machine is paid for. Is that a fair offer?
Could I afford to send this Self-Working Washer on a full month's trial, at my own expense for freight, if there was any trick in this offer?
How could I make any money out of this kind of offer if the Washer wouldn't do all that I say it will?
Will you try our Self-Working Washer a month at my expense?
If you haven't got running water in your house, I'll tell you how this Washer can be worked without it.
Drop me a line today for further particulars.
Address R. F. Bieber, Treasurer 1900 Washer Co., 5050 Henry Street, Binghamton, N. Y.

49. Advertisement for one of the recently invented washing machines, c. 1885.

as once a week at least." Colored tablecloths instead of white could serve for extended periods of time, and mothers were advised to make their children wear bibs; "if these are of rubber they need not go in the wash."[23]

The washing machine was an innovation of the post–Civil War era that did not enjoy immediate adulation. The nineteenth-century washing machine was essentially a washtub on a stand with a flywheel-driven set of beaters or paddles that agitated the clothes. Early washers evidently tore clothes and left rust spots (from the bolts used to fasten parts together) and often leaked. The Sears Roebuck Company offered several varieties of the washing machine in 1902, priced from $2.72 to $5.62. They guaranteed that their machines would not damage clothing.[24] The capacity of these machines was generally five or six shirts—a significant number for a society that changed collars and cuffs more often than entire shirts, and advocated changing undergarments "as often as once a week at least." By 1910 combination washer-wringers with greater capacities were available and had become almost as popular as sewing machines (Fig. 49). They lessened the difficult physical labor of scrubbing and wringing.

With or without a machine, washing and drying generally occupied an entire day. On the following day, collars, cuffs, bed and table linens, shirt fronts, skirts, and miscellaneous personal linens were ironed. The process required at least two different types of iron: a coarse iron, which was roughly triangular, and a polishing iron, which was rounded on both ends. More specialized shapes and weights were available, and the efficient home had more than one of each, so that one could be heating on the stove while the other was being used (Fig. 50). Ironing was done in the kitchen, either on a surface temporarily wrapped with flannel or on a "bosom board," a small board (usually eight to ten inches by eighteen to twenty-four inches) covered with cotton and flannel. Cuffs, collars, and shirt fronts were usually dipped in starch before ironing. Ironing occupied an entire day, and seems to have been hired out whenever possible.[25]

Like cooking and laundry, cleaning the home in late-nineteenth-century America had daily, weekly, and seasonal rhythms. Diary and journal accounts by women reveal that daily maintenance cleaning included sweeping

50. The variety of ironing tools patented, manufactured, and used in the nineteenth century is nearly endless. Complicated clothing made washing and ironing drudgery, but crimpers and fluters were helpful for ironing voluminous ruffles. Above: crimper, cast iron and brass. North Brothers Manufacturing Company, Philadelphia, 1877–1890. Below, right, top: crimper, cast iron. Geneva Hand Crimper Manufacturing Company, Geneva, Illinois, c. 1870. Below, right, bottom: sleeve iron, cast iron. American, 1870–1900. All other irons are of cast iron. American, 1870–1900.

51. The inexpensive and efficient carpet sweeper was hailed as a woman's savior. Wood and painted metal. Bissell Carpet Sweeper Company, Grand Rapids, Michigan, 1873–1899.

the kitchen, dusting, cleaning and filling lamps, washing dishes, and making beds. Parlors, studies, halls, and stairways were swept twice weekly—on Friday or Saturday, in preparation for the Sabbath, and, if laundry was hired out, on Monday. Saturday, therefore, could be a day as full of chores as the weekdays, especially because baking and cooking had to be done for both Saturday and Sunday. Almira MacDonald tersely wrote in 1870: "busy fixing for Sabbath as usual on Saturday."[26]

Sweeping rugs, according to a columnist in *The Household*, was "the hardest torture of the week, . . . prosecuted until every nerve is throbbing in fierce rebellion at the undue pressure to which it is subjected."[27] The carpet sweeper (Fig. 51) was one of the most efficient technological innovations of the nineteenth century, and it has remained virtually unchanged since it first appeared. The sweeper was composed of two brushes mounted on the axles of its wheels. The brushes swept dirt up into the encasement as the machine was pushed or pulled over the rug.

The early vacuum cleaner (Fig. 52) was a less successful alternative to hand-sweeping rugs. When the vacuum cleaner piston was pumped up and down in the cylinder, a partial vacuum was created, lifting dirt off the rug. Advertised as the "new servant in the house," vacuum cleaners ironically required more effort and were more expensive than carpet sweepers—vacuum cleaner prices ranged from $4.15 in the 1911 Sears Roebuck catalog to $16.50 for the "Dust Filler" model. The vacuum cleaner became truly labor-saving only when it was electrified, after the turn of the century, and no longer required arduous hand-pumping.

One advantage of labor-saving devices was that they helped eliminate the need for domestic servants, who by 1910 were becoming difficult to find. In an article in *Outlook*, a popular magazine of the early twentieth century, Martha Bruere characterized "The New Home-Making" as joyously free of hired help: "The last year I have kept no maid, having discharged my last one after nearly six years of service, and have enjoyed the year more than the previous one. . . . I never hesitate to spend money for any labor-saving device."[28]

Consistent with their charge to maintain an ordered and healthy environment, each spring and autumn Victorian women participated in the ritual of total housecleaning. Cities and towns in the nineteenth century were probably dirtier than those of the present. Many streets were unpaved, and dust and horse manure were constant problems in the summer months. Oil and gas lamps left residues, and coal grates were sources of soot and ash. Spring housecleaning, usually during the last two weeks in April, generally included removing carpets for cleaning, washing windows and floors, organizing closets, packing winter clothes, removing winter stoves, cleaning the furnace (if there was one), painting walls and floors (especially those of the kitchen), and cleaning pantries, upholstered furniture, bins, beds, and bedsteads. Mrs. E. Clayton Smith, an instructor in painting and the wife of a physician in Honeyoe Falls, a small village in upstate New York, recorded a typical list of housecleaning tasks:

> Monday, April 16 [1883]: I cleaned some upstairs in the morning. . . . I raked some in the yard at night.
> Monday, April 23: I cleaned the parlour and the bedroom off the sitting room.
> Tuesday, April 24: I put up my plush lambrequin in the parlour.
> Tuesday, May 1: I cleaned my kitchen.
> Thursday, May 3: I began painting my kitchen floor.
> Saturday, May 12: Cleaned my sitting room. Stove was moved out in the morning.[29]

Smith reconvened her painting class on May 16. The Smiths apparently had neither children nor domestic help. Dr. Smith was one of the few physicians within a twenty-five-mile radius of their home, and spent most of his time traveling, leaving Mrs. Smith to tend their house and garden alone.

52. Early vacuum cleaners were neither efficient nor inexpensive. The labor involved in pumping the piston made this innovation more important as a status symbol than as a workable tool. Wood and painted metal. Hugro Manufacturing Company, Warsaw, Indiana, 1911.

In the city, spring cleaning was an equally big project. The MacDonald family paid a woman to help take up the carpets for cleaning. Like Dr. Smith, Mr. MacDonald, an attorney, traveled extensively, and Mrs. MacDonald handled the massive spring cleaning alone.

> Saturday, April 25 Busy cleaning Arthur's room, arranging both that and mine. . . . Anne went nearly all day after arbutus, returned tired. Mother and I out on errands after tea, and I went into Mrs. Greenleaf's a while. I baked a cake.
> Tuesday, May 5: Stained the hall floor edges and took up carpet, back chamber; am suffering this afternoon with griping pains.

On May 2, 1870, exactly fifteen years earlier, MacDonald "had two women here to clean house, one all day; took up two parlour and dining room carpets . . . very tired." The following day, she finished housecleaning with one of the hired women.[30]

Autumn housecleaning did not commence as regularly as the spring project, varying from mid-October to mid-December. Houses were again completely cleaned, stoves reinstalled, and wood and coal secured and stored for winter. Susan Hooker described the process to her mother in a letter of December 8, 1878:

> We took up the carpet and sent it out to be cleaned with steam and brushes. It will cost two dollars, but it is dirty and so full of fever. . . . Feathers renovated, blankets, comforters, ticks washed, [I] picked over the hair from my two mattresses, and the two cribs, and tied them again, and made a mattress for the boy's new bedstead. Our only outlay was thirty-seven cents for having the feathers renovated and the buying [of] the boy's bedstead.[31]

The yearly cycle of work in the home included other unscheduled chores such as mattress-cleaning, rug-mending, furniture-cushioning, and, in the words of Lydia Maria

Child, "innumerable jobs too small to be mentioned."[32]

Sewing was the most frequently recorded domestic labor performed by middle-class women. They sewed their everyday working clothes, their undergarments, blouses, bonnets, pillowcases, towels, and handkerchiefs (Fig. 53), as well as their grand dresses. They also made most of their husbands' and sons' clothing, especially shirts, cuffs, and collars. Many women knitted socks, stockings, scarves, and other assorted woolen gear for the winter.

Women obtained information about clothing styles from "fashion plates" in popular magazines. The women depicted in these prints were engaged in formal social activity, and the clothing shown was appropriate only for such occasions. The ankle-length skirts, voluminous and heavy, were suspended from a severely cinched waist, and the tight-fitting bodices, almost always of a heavy, woven

53. Sewing tools were often elaborate and beautiful. Top row, from left: scissors, sheet steel and wood, possibly German, c. 1870–1910; wood, ivory, and velvet sewing box, American, c. 1875; molded steel sewing clamps, American, c. 1860–1880. Bottom row, from left: pincushions, silver plate and velvet, Lister and Sons, Newcastle, England, c. 1872; cast-steel scissors, possibly German, 1870–1920; cast-steel tape measures, American, c. 1910; steel, plastic, and cotton tape measures, German, c. 1880–1920. Hand-embroidered linens, stamped "Sarah Sharp" and "Emily Blackburn." American, c. 1885.

material, covered the arms to the wrist, even in summer. Women always wore hats in these images. Periodicals also included instructions on "making over" old dresses—reversing materials, relining skirts, replacing trimming, and combining salvageable parts of two or more outfits into one. Throughout the last thirty-five years of the nineteenth century, the Huntingtons, for example, regularly remade "cast-off" skirts and "drawers" into "comely ones."[33]

Often a dressmaker, almost always a married woman who needed extra income for her own family, came to a woman's home to help her cut out and stitch garments for about a dollar a day. Relatives, friends, and neighbors also helped, as the Huntington women's letters indicate:

> Was so excited with the thought of the amount of sewing I had to do that I was awake at daylight. . . . Mrs. Corkill working with me all week. Julia Gritten [a neighbor] is helping with her machine.

> I thought if Sue is to do the housekeeping, I would assist her in making her clothes so this week I have fixed her cloth dress and spotted merino and now we shall endeavor to do Kate's dress . . . and finish Carrie's black dress. I suppose Frank's clothes all will need some call and your Father must have some shirts made as soon as we can get to them.

> I became interested in making Bert's clothes and have kept on. Fannie Hooker [a relative] helps me baste and Fannie Gay [a friend] stitches so I have cut out over thirty garments this week.[34]

The bulk of the dressmaking was done in the winter and spring months. Almira MacDonald worked with her hired dressmaker two days a week during May and June, commencing her work as soon as spring cleaning was complete. Women skilled in the needle trades were evidently in great demand. On ten separate occasions between May 8 and June 23, 1870, MacDonald, for example, employed at least one dressmaker or seamstress. She also filled the three weeks between the end of fall housecleaning and Thanksgiving with intensive sewing, hiring a dressmaker six times between October 26 and November 19.[35]

The sewing machine (Fig. 54) was probably the most significant domestic labor-saving device in the late nineteenth century. In 1860 a series of articles in *Godey's* characterized it as "The Queen of Inventions," and credited it with relieving the drudgery of the "pale woman plying her sickly trade," an amelioration that "philanthropy failed to accomplish, and that religion, poetry, eloquence and reason had sought in vain."

> The *Sewing Machine* will, after a time, effectually banish ragged and unclad humanity from every class. . . . In all Benevolent Institutions these machines are now in

54. The "Queen of Inventions." Sewing machine, cast iron and wood. S. M. White Company, New York, c. 1885.

operation, and do, or may do, a hundred times more towards clothing the indigent and feeble than the united fingers of all the charitable and willing ladies collected through the civilized would could possibly perform. . . . [And for the] wealthier homes of our land . . . the Sewing Machine is a treasure. Instead of busy fingers and vacant minds, young ladies . . . can have the opportunity of improving their minds . . . while aiding their mothers in all the sewing for the family.[36]

The exuberant response to the introduction of this invention, even though it cost between fifty and seventy-five dollars in 1860, indicates the huge quantity of sewing women did in the late nineteenth century. As *Godey's* described: "We have no conception of the rapidity with which machines are being introduced into families and manufactories. . . . We found [Wheeler and Wilson's] ample rooms thronged with visitors and purchasers." *Godey's* continued its celebration of the sewing machine with a brief article which contained a table of comparative work times for machine- and hand-sewn garments. A gentleman's shirt required one hour and sixteen minutes by machine and fourteen hours and twenty-six minutes by hand; a chemise, one hour and one minute by machine and ten hours and thirty-one minutes by hand. The figures may be somewhat suspect, because they were provided by the Wheeler and Wilson Sewing Machine Company, but even modified, they would be impressive.[37]

To overcome the obstacle of the high price, *Godey's* editors suggested that six to ten families pool their resources, buy a machine, and form a "sewing machine club." This arrangement would provide ten families with the use of the machine for "thirty-one working days of the year."[38] Diaries of the period suggest that women who had machines frequently lent them to friends without.

In addition to liberating women to enrich their minds with other pursuits, the sewing machine was heralded as the beginning of a new age of education in the mechanical arts for women.

The general introduction [of sewing machines] would do more to diffuse knowledge of mechanical powers, than could be accomplished by any other possible method. Not only would wives and daughters become enlightened upon a subject now dark to them, but the boys under their charge, the men in miniature, would have their curiosity aroused in contact with the finest and most effective . . . of machinery of modern times.[39]

Dressmaking was ambiguously linked with mental, moral, and physical health in the late nineteenth century. Not working was unconscionable. Idle or "lazy" women were "miserable," according to *Godey's,* but too much work, especially needlework, made life "nothing but a dull round of everlasting toil, and too often have eyesight and health, as well as hope and spirits, sunk under the burden." The sewing machine originally promised to ease that burden, but the power of "fashion" and "vanity fair" prompted some women to further embellish their clothes, striving for the appearance of wealth. As women's rights advocate Antoinette Brown Blackwell contended: "Genius can make its own place honorable; but this seems infinitely harder to the great body of womanhood. As an alternative they double the time required in making each garment and quadruple it by altering over each old one, tempting their already overworked sisters into the same destructive fashion seeking." Dress-reform activist Abba Gould Woolson criticized women "who yet cannot afford to hire their dressmaking" for "desiring to appear more wealthy than they really are." In her opinion, "led by false pride to conceal the fact that they are their own dressmakers," they are kept "in the house plying the needle," deprived of "daily outdoor exercises."[40]

Thus, women were faced with an ideological and practical dilemma. They were citicized in periodicals for being slaves to the capricious fashions of a French courtly tradition, yet encouraged to follow those trends both by the fashion plates in those same magazines and by the ready availability of paper patterns by the 1880s (Fig. 55).

They were similarly confronted with a set of cultural values that glorified them as women because of their refined skills in needlework while attacking them for striving to appear wealthy beyond their actual means. If the "blood and treasure" required to produce goods declined, and what had once been the mark of high status became available to the masses (or at least the middle class), how was the elite to maintain distance from the rank-and-file? One answer was to criticize those who used their new-found time to ape the rich, thus setting up an order of decorative restraint for the middle class which did not apply to the wealthy. When the attempt to impose this ideological position on the middle and lower classes failed, it was adopted instead by the upper class as a "reform" style, and thus as a new canon of "good taste." The late-nineteenth-century popularity of "English reform" or Eastlake furniture and furnishings is in part explained by this ideological pattern. Charles Locke Eastlake's *Hints on Household Taste* was first published in the United States in 1872, four years after it had appeared in England. It was an immediate success, and the flat, planar, and relatively unornamented style was quickly produced and successfully marketed as a tasteful reaction against the "excesses" of Renaissance or French styles.

Critics of labor-saving devices were certainly a minority in the panoply of advice for homemakers, but their often strident voices reflect a broad conservative strain of thinking about home, work, and the nation. In "Some Thoughts on the Completed Century," in the January 1876 issue of *Godey's*, Mrs. Hopkinson wrote:

Here, especially in our cities, we turn a crank and water flows; we turn another and a full coal-hod rises from the cellar; another turn and hot air pours up from a glowing furnace. Machinery washes our clothes; we pass them through a clothes wringer, they dry in a hot drying room, and somebody turns a mangle. Somehow the forces of nature are brought to bear in a way to save moving a muscle . . . (for in these days your sewing is

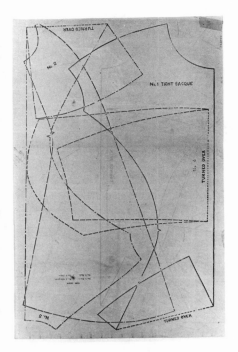

55. These patterns appear to be much more complicated than those of the present. To obtain separate pieces to pin to fabric, a seamstress had to trace them first on separate sheets of paper. Butterick Manufacturing Company, New York, c. 1890.

done by machine, and who is going to knit when there are knitting machines?).

Mechanization was causing the deterioration of the American woman's health.

> Women of the present day labor under the disadvantage of being placed where most of the comforts of life are to be obtained without physical effort, and this fact has probably been at the root of the deterioration of bodily strength which is the common observance of travellers in regard to American women.[41]

A woman was urged to have her daughters "work with her . . . learning the whole round of the neat housekeeper's duties. When this is done . . . we may expect better housekeepers, made from well-developed girls—women with muscles, bones, and nerves—with a smaller number of the victims of that freakish and horrid disease, neuralgia, and, as a natural and legitimate result, a healthier, wiser, and happier race."[42]

The 1876 centennial celebration helped sharpen the focus of critics of the new domestic technology. Comparisons to "our grandmothers" abound in the advice literature of the last quarter of the nineteenth century, and the modern woman always pales in comparison to the noble helpmate of a century before. As Dr. J. N. Hanaford wrote in *The Household* in 1881: "Our grandmothers—worthy companions of the Puritans—transformed the wool produced on the farm, and the flax, into fabrics, and garments even, by their skill, and did their own housework, few of them having 'help.' Those were the days of simplicity."[43] His initial assumption—that "our grandmothers" were all of Puritan stock—reflects the ideological core of the popular late-nineteenth-century interest in the people and artifacts of the American colonial era. Cultural decline, manifest in the ill health of women or in the labor unrest and changing immigration patterns of the late nineteenth century, became a topic of discussion and analysis among the

Anglo-Saxon elite. Their veneration of the colonial era was expressed in a burgeoning of "colonial" or "pilgrim" trademarks on everything from carpet sweepers to processed foods, furniture which allegedly replicated that of the seventeenth or eighteenth century, and the transformation of the tools and household wares of the early settlers into relics.[44]

Anxiety about maintaining WASP supremacy and preserving the distinction between classes may explain why the use of hired labor for domestic tasks was not summoned as evidence of the decline of American women, though labor-saving devices often were. The obvious status implied by the ability to pay a domestic servant exempted from criticism the many middle-class women who accomplished their domestic chores with some form of paid assistance.[45] Middle-class homes were often too large for one woman to keep as clean and orderly as the upstanding wife and mother ought, so live-in or daily help was often part of the lifestyle.

Kate Huntington Taylor of Connecticut and Carolyn T. Lyon of Rochester, New York, expressed their pleasure at having domestic help:

I . . . expect a dressmaker for the latter part of the week. My girl is taking hold nicely and doesn't need to be told a thing twice. She washed very well last week, and Mrs. Brenel taught her to iron starched clothes, and is coming this week to give her another lesson. I have finished up the little cleaning that wasn't done, and have realized more fully all that I have escaped.

You will be glad to hear that we have a gem of a second girl, and tomorrow brings a new cook, so my domestic labors are diminishing, though the responsibility is on the increase.[46]

Nonetheless, domestic service by no means allowed women of the middle class to become "managers" of a home. The more common situation was a division of labor.

Almira MacDonald had one servant for most of the post–
Civil War era, and generally did the sewing and baking
herself and then helped her servant with housecleaning.
Susan Huntington Hooker wrote her mother: "Maggie
and I get along splendidly. She takes care of all the back
part of the house, upstairs and down, cleans the lamps,
and does all the cleaning I want done in here, and takes
the baby whenever I want her to do so."[47] The notion
of the "lady" who becomes a "manager" and is then
freed to engage in charitable service work is the ideal, as
evoked in such proselytizing works as Catherine Beecher's
Treatise on Domestic Economy (1847) and *Domestic Receipt Book* (1846), but it was not the reality of middle-
class life.

Though some middle-class households could afford to
employ domestic servants, others were victims of the increased demand for servants which was not met by a
similar increase in the number of women willing to work
as domestics. The number of female domestics doubled
between 1870 and 1910 (from 960,000 to 1,830,000),
but demand, according to historian David Katzman, increased at a greater rate. Between 1880 and 1920, the
number of servants and laundresses per one thousand
northeastern families declined steadily. In Boston the number dropped from 239 to 82; in New York from 217 to
74; in Buffalo from 157 to 55, and in Philadelphia from
203 to 81. Statistics for the percentage of homes employing
at least one live-in domestic servant during the period from
1870 to 1910 are uneven and scattered, and vary from
city to city in the Northeast, but twenty-five percent seems
a safe figure. Gwendolyn Wright estimates that in the late
nineteenth century twenty to twenty-five percent of Chicago households employed live-in servants, and the work
of Virginia McLaughlin, David Katzman, and Faye Dudden confirms this estimate.[48] The new industrial equiva-
lents of housework—food processing, laundry, and the
garment industry—offered better wages than domestic employers, and attracted many of the men and women who
might have been servants ten or twenty years earlier.

The characteristic employer-employee relationship was contentious, and both employers and employees were advised to be considerate and tolerant. Josiah Gilbert Holland warned women to remember that "servants are human beings . . . with rights no amount of service money can buy; . . . transcendent intellectual endowments, a physical development of fifty-horse power, the broad circle of the Christian graces and virtues, a faultless disposition, a knowledge of French cookery, and elegant habits, cannot be obtained for nine Yankee shillings a week." Catherine Beecher urged domestics to "remember that you can never find a place in this world where everything will be just as you want it, and that it is a bad thing for you, as well as for your employer, to keep moving about from one place to another. Stay where you are, and try to make those things that trouble you more tolerable, by enduring them with patience."[49] In fact, few domestic servants were likely to read this or any other treatise concerned with their job.

Americans had been ambivalent about geographic mobility for all citizens—not just servants or laborers—since the seventeenth century.[50] Many nineteenth-century Americans associated the propensity to stay in motion with the advance of the democratic ethos and the health of the economy. But for others geographic mobility had a disruptive influence. Training new employees, whether in the mills or the home, took time. "We have a young and inexperienced girl in our kitchen," Alcesta Huntington complained, "and all my time is given to helping things move there." Her sister wrote of similar difficulties: "My tribulations with domestics still continue and each one is worse than the one who went before. I average a change once every two weeks, so you will see my horizon has been necessarily small as it seems to be all I can do to keep things running." Two weeks later, she wrote: "I have [sic] a new girl come today who promises better than anything I have had yet. I just got rid of the fourth nuisance since August."[51]

The longer a household could keep a competent and

placid domestic servant, the more economical the situation would be for the employer. It is clear, then, that, as Beecher contended, it was a "bad thing" for the employer if the servant worked for a short time and left, but it is not clear why this was a "bad thing" for the employee. Beecher quite naturally expressed the ideology of her class. To put it another way, mobility was a good thing for the middle class, but a "bad thing" for the working class.

The extent of the bitterness between mistresses and servants is nowhere more evident than in the transcripts, albeit edited by the woman employer, of the rows that took place. In a letter to her mother, Alcesta Huntington described the termination of their cook:

> I asked Norah why his table was not made ready for him. Norah gave me to understand that she did not consider it her business and that Libbie was expected to do it. I told her Libbie had nothing to do with it, that it was kitchen work and belonged to the cook. She said she would not do it and we must get some one else.[52]

More violent was the following dismissal from the MacDonald home in 1885:

> Not willing to cook what was needed she said she would go and I acquiesced. Then when asked if she would have time to work—before—she refused . . . she had been paid nearly up . . . [yet] when told Mr. MacD[onald] would settle at his office . . . she said she would not go a step after it, but would stay another week and do nothing. . . . [He] paid her all but 50 cents which he deducted for breaking many articles when mad. She allowed she would not leave until every cent was given. He ordered her out and she threw the money, six and ½ silver doll[ar]s on the table, he said he would put her out. Then she started and he locked the door and put her trunk in the lattice. . . . I went to the office too. I was nervous and thought it best to.[53]

The causes for these traumatic episdoes lay in the complex emotional nexus of master-servant relationships. Employers tended to regard domestics as objects or commodities, and often assumed they could dictate the most intimate aspects of the servant's life. For example, in 1880 Kate Taylor wrote from Connecticut to her mother in Rochester, New York, that her present servant "will be married next Sat[urday]: if [the new woman being trained is] not satisfactory, she will have to stay and teach another." When her domestic became pregnant, Carrie Jessup insisted that the "girl" give up either her baby or her job. "I still have my girl . . . but it is quite uncertain for how long. I know if she has her baby, I do not want her, for the very time that I want her the most she has to attend to the baby. She has written to her friends in Boston to get a boarding place for the baby, and if they succeed will remain with me, but if not will go."[54]

The mistress-servant relationship was complicated by the ideological tension between home and commerce in the late nineteenth century: the middle-class home was supposed to be a sanctuary from the evils of the world of commerce and labor, yet domestic servants brought commercial labor into the home. In most cases, servants were alone, in situations of often intense ethnic, class, or racial hostility. They were often disparagingly called "Bridgets," referring to the preponderance of Irish natives who entered the service of Anglo-Saxon Protestant mistresses. Josiah Gilbert Holland warned mothers:

> Beware of trusting an infant, too confidingly, to a European nurse . . . she may take it into dirty alleys, on a visit to some of her own relations, perhaps newly arrived in an emigrant ship, with the filth and diseases of a steerage passage still about them. . . . Or, believing it a meritorious act, an Irish nurse may secretly carry the infant to a priest, and have it baptised in the Catholic church, herself standing godmother. . . . Above all, do not permit your own children to play with the children of their nurse. No good ever accrues from it.[55]

So the live-in servant was separated from her own family, living and working among families who were economically more advantaged and who considered themselves morally and racially superior to her. She worked between eighty and one hundred hours per week, with only one afternoon and part or all of Sunday off. Yet this time-off was not guaranteed, and was often illusory. "My servant is hired to do whatever she is told to do and to be at any time subject to my command" was the credo of the employer, in this case stated before a federal commission investigating labor in 1900.[56] The servant's only recourse in an untenable situation was to seek other work, and when given the alternative of factory work in the late nineteenth century, many women turned to the industrial sector. According to historian Virginia McLaughlin, Kate Taylor's experience in 1880 was becoming more and more common: "I received a letter in reply to one I had written Sarah about her sister. She thinks she will keep on in the factory, so I must look elsewhere."[57] The expansion of the industrial sector of the American economy that had helped produce the middle class ironically worked to remove one of its symbols of success—the domestic servant.

Factory work was more appealing than domestic service for several reasons. The hours were usually shorter, and the pay, however meager, was better. Moreover, women in factories were in the company of many other women, rather than alone or with one or two other people like themselves. Domestic service may have given them more pleasant surroundings in which to work, but it also was a constant reminder of class differences. In addition, the enormous cultural responsibility placed upon a servant's employer—to be both stewardess of the home and moral guardian—without the power to effect that charge, inevitably meant that the servant was the scapegoat for those frustrating times when the woman of the house fell short of social expectations.

Help in her labors—machines and gadgets, domestic servants, hired-out labor, or children—eased women's workloads somewhat in the late nineteenth century, but never liberated them from their chores altogether. It mattered little, moreover, whether a woman was wealthy or middle-class: idleness was a vice, and work of some sort was a virtue. Thus, the few fortunate women who were essentially free of traditional forms of housework, as well as their counterparts of the middle class, were expected to turn their liberated energies not to leisure, but to more work, thereby enriching their domestic environment.

In the latter half of the nineteenth century, the "ideal" home for the middle-class family was the free-standing suburban house. This form of housing—where men lived but did not work—began to be built extensively after the Civil War, when there was both a sizable middle class that could afford the investment and a rapid and inexpensive means for these wage-earners to travel into the urban centers where they worked. The urban growth and industrialization of the middle decades of the nineteenth century brought with them a parallel increase in the number of managers, bureaucrats, and other employees not directly connected to the productive sector. In addition, the development of the streetcar and the trolley enabled the middle-class family to translate the money from a managerial position into a house and land isolated from the commercial, vice-ridden world of the city. Urban apartment living appealed to some middle-class Americans, but, for most of them, the model living situation was the one-family house. The mother and children stayed at home, and the father went off to work each day.

This home was to be the opposite of the man's world; rather than an environment that bespoke commerce and trade, it was a miniature universe of culture and education for family and visitors. Here the arts and sciences of the museum, concert hall, and schoolroom were translated into the shells and other curios adorning the parlor, the prints and paintings on the walls, the piano or organ in the parlor, and the books in the library. Women were the organizing force and marshals of this domain. Defined as more emotional and sensitive than their male counterparts, they were charged with transforming the rude brick, stone, and wood of the exterior and the blank walls and empty rooms of the interior into places which would both communicate a family's status and provide it with repose and moral uplift.

The style of interior decoration in the late nineteenth century was emblematic of the separate realms and responsibilities of middle-class life. Visual complexity and intricacy characterized popular decorative taste in the

FOUR

DECORATING
THE HOME

home, as could be seen in both the massing of discrete objects in a given space and the juxtaposing of different patterns and textures. This celebration of asymmetry and visual surprise served as more than mere display of worldly goods: it was an evocative and feminine counterpoint to the increasingly bureaucratic, machined-straight lives of middle-class men. The volume and variety of objects and textures in a typical house, when properly arranged, were supposed to alter immoral and unchristian behavior by the power of "influence," rather than by direct confrontation. The woman's "sphere of influence" was passive and limited, both by her culturally prescribed role as helpmate and by her husband's control of the family's finances. His economic power placed her in a position of dependency.

Women looking for information about decorating walls, covering floors, and choosing appropriate furniture for the various rooms in the house could find it in books and popular women's magazines of the period. *Godey's, Peterson's,* and *The Household* included monthly columns which solicited homemaking advice from their subscribers, and major publishing houses issued a continuous stream of books like Harriet Spofford's *Art Decoration Applied to Furniture* (1879) throughout the latter half of the nineteenth century.

The front entrance hall was the most obviously public space in the house, and an area of critical importance. It was a visitor's introduction to a home, and its decor was the first key to the character of both the dwelling and its inhabitants. Light colors were recommended for painted wall surfaces, and a dado (a band of wallpaper or wooden wainscoting) and rail were often installed to protect the lower three feet of the wall surface. Following the directions included in inexpensive decorating books, women could stencil designs above the dado rail. Stenciling was considered superior to machine-printed wallpaper by many decorating advisors because colors could be modulated for variety of tone, eliminating what some critics viewed as the monotony of repetitive wallpaper patterns.

The upper section of the typical hall door included a

window, and some door enframements contained side windows which allowed more light to enter the hall. By the 1870s stained glass was mass-produced and inexpensive, and was often used in hall doors and windows to add a rich, decorative note. It also carried connotations of religion and morality, making the vestibule into a kind of vestry for the sanctified family within.

The vast majority of middle-class homes had narrow entry halls, and a hall tree or hall stand (Fig. 56) was the dominant decorative feature of the space, providing a place for hats, coats, walking sticks, and umbrellas. Almost all forms had a seat and a mirror, which not only reflected light, but assured individuals of their appearance before entering either the mannered space of the parlor or the public arena of the outside. If the hall stand was not equipped with a seat, a straight chair was usually provided for people to put on overshoes and for messengers or servants to rest while waiting.

Another important furnishing of the entrance hall was a card-receiver, placed on a small table or on the hall tree shelf (Fig. 57). The hall was thus an intermediate space, where one could make social intentions known without face-to-face contact, preserve the privacy of the domestic

56. Many hall stands had decorative elements with religious motifs, a signal to visitors that a Christian family lived within. Equipped with a pan and arms to hold umbrellas, as well as a central mirror so that visitors could adjust their appearance, this hall tree embodies both the cross and the quatrefoil. Wood, mirrored glass, and cast iron. American, c. 1880.

57. The silver-plated card receiver was an important front hall decoration, a symbol of the owner's taste and hospitality. Meriden Britannia Company, Meriden, Connecticut, c. 1885.

circle from intrusion by the working class, prepare one's visage and demeanor for social interaction, and store over-clothes without cluttering the carefully constructed decor of the parlor.

From the entrance hall, guests were ushered into the room that served as the main social area of the home. "Whether as drawing-room or parlor," wrote Mary Gay Humphreys in 1896, "this room should convey a sense of elegance, good taste, recognition of the polite arts, and of graceful, social amenities."[1] Parlors reflected the family's wealth, dignity, and cultural development. They also symbolized both the closeness of the family group and its social communion with friends. Since the parlor generally served as a formal family gathering place, it was decorated to be instructive as well as attractive. Historical or religious prints, figurines, plants, flowers, and treasured mementos were placed on walls and mantels (Fig. 58). Etagères, the Victorian "museums" in the home, where a family displayed decorative artifacts and natural objects such as

58. Prints with pious sentiments were common in middle-class homes of the late nineteenth century. "The Boy Preacher," by J. W. Venable, pencil and ink on paper. American, c. 1870.

shells, were a domestic manifestation of the nineteenth-century urge to collect and classify the exotic and the curious (Fig. 59).

Popular since the 1850s, matched sets of parlor furniture—usually a sofa, a gentleman's chair, a side chair, and a lady's chair—reflected both the canons of appropriate behavior in the parlor and the nature of ideal family structure. Gentleman's chairs were akin to thrones. They were always higher than lady's chairs, and the high backs and arms signified that men were expected to lean back and be comfortable (Fig. 60). Lady's chairs had no arms, and thus no visible means of bracing and support for the chair

59. Owned by a moderately prosperous attorney in a small town, this étagère was stocked with all the accessories of a cultured home. The library is represented by the books on the lower shelves; the art gallery, by the printed glass and ceramic wares; the natural world, by the shellwork. Copy of an original photograph of an étagère in the parlor of a house in Victor, New York, c. 1880.

back. Armlessness allowed space for women's skirts and multitudinous petticoats, but also asserted the era's posture requirements for women—upright, away from the chair back, with their hands folded in their lap. The idea of a set or "suite" of identically styled but gender-distinctive furniture signified the separate but organically related "spheres" of ideal family life. Social practice and material form were one.

Many homes of the post–Civil War period had both a furnace and a fireplace; the latter was sometimes gas-fired or installed without any intention of use for heat. Though furnaces had replaced fireplaces as the source of heat, they were still a symbol of warmth. Here the family gathered in the traditional way, expressing the values with which the hearth had been associated—trust, interdependence, and safety.[2] The hearth was also significant as a zone for decorative tiles or display on or above mantels.

The center table was an alternate gathering spot for the family (Fig. 61). Lighted from above by a fixture hung from the center of the ceiling or by a portable lamp, this table first came into use in the 1840s. It was especially significant in homes without fireplaces.

Women of the late nineteenth century often made small covers for their furniture, both to soften angular lines and

60. The high backs and arms on men's chairs allowed men to lean back and be comfortable. Women's chairs had no arms, in part to accommodate their full skirts. "Ladies'" and "gentlemen's" chairs, mahogany with horsehair upholstery. American, c. 1860–1885.

61. This lithograph reinforces the idea of the male as commander of the family unit. "Reading the Scriptures," by Benjamin Robert Haydon. New York, 1852.

to protect finishes or upholstery. Mantels, corner brackets, easels, pianos, chair backs, windows, and shelves were often adorned and protected with sewn covers made of everything from inexpensive muslin and colored calico to plain sateen or coarse silk trimmed with macramé lace at top and bottom (Fig. 62). Lambrequins (Fig. 63), the horizontal borders of fabric which were draped over the tops of windows, doors, shelves, and mantels, relieved what Janet Ruutz-Rees, in *Home Decoration* (1881), called the "ugliness" of furnishings, "sometimes constructed of the commonest material, and almost always of unsightly shape and harsh outline." In her opinion: "The sooner [they are] covered up the better." She favored lambrequins with a quiet, conventional design against a neutral background, and suggested that the effect would be heightened by carrying a matching piece of fabric up the face of the chimney. This was either "arranged in folds, or hung from rings upon a brass rod," forming a background for objects displayed on the mantel shelf.[3] Vases and plaques were thought to be especially attractive placed in such a setting. After 1885, when people began to associate light and air

EMBROIDERY FOR END OF PIANO-SCARF OR STOOL.

62. Commercially printed patterns like this
one made the social requirement of
artistic needlework a little easier to meet,
but also removed some of the individual
creativity involved. Pattern for a piano scarf,
supplement to *Peterson's Magazine*,
New York, 1890.

with health, lambrequins became unacceptable because
they were stationary and excluded light from the top of
the window. Lambrequins were often replaced by valances,
which could easily be pushed aside.

Textiles recycled into decorative pieces demonstrated a
woman's frugality and artistic skill. Remnants of rich fabrics—satins, velvets, and silks—were reused in decorative
quilts made for display in the parlor. Called "crazy quilts"
because of the irregular shapes of the patches sewn together, the finished pieces often had painted pictures and
colorful embroidery (Fig. 64). Linen sheets, when too
worn-out for the bedchamber, were embroidered to make
tidies, napkins, and tray cloths; and old curtains were
sometimes recycled as cushions. These activities and virtues
were expected of all women, not just those with limited
means. Almira MacDonald's family had a position of some
importance, yet she noted in 1895 that her daughter Nan
was "fixing pillows for corner . . . sofas. She stuffed [the]
cushions with straw or hay and covered [them] with
woolen curtains."[4]

Skill in embroidery was also both a statement of a woman's artistic talents and a measure of her ability to decorate
without great expense. It was particularly recommended
for chair backs, cushions, table covers, doilies, and the
ubiquitous antimacassars or tidies. These were small pro-
tective coverings attached to the backs of chairs or sofas
to protect the plain or embroidered coverings from the
hairgrooming pomades favored by nineteenth-century
men. Easily removed for laundering, they could also be an
annoyance: "Nothing irritates an unfortunate man more
than the inevitable disposition that tidies have to stick to
his broadcloth! and nothing gives a more untidy look to
a room than these same 'tidies' when out of place."[5]

The dining room was perhaps as important as the parlor,
since it was where the often public and mannered ritual
of eating occurred. One correspondent for *The Household*
suggested that young wives "get everything you need for
the kitchen and dining room, even if you have to wait a
little while before furnishing your parlor." Because two or

three times a day "it is the family rendezvous," Mary Gay Humphreys remarked, "it should be the most cheerful and most enjoyable room in the house."[6] Painted walls or wainscoting, rather than wallpaper, were recommended, since the latter absorbed food odors, was difficult to clean, and was therefore thought to create an unpleasant and unhealthy atmosphere in the room. For the same reasons, leather or rush, rather than velvet, mohair plush, or tapestry, was recommended for the seats of dining room chairs (Fig. 65). A sideboard, a serving table, and a screen to hide the pantry door were other essentials in the fashionable

63. Decorative pieces, often constructed of velvet or felt, were intended to "soften" the hard lines of machine-made furniture. Lambrequin, felt with silk and wool embroidery appliqué. American, c. 1870.

64. Crazy quilts were used for decoration, rarely for warmth. Testaments to a woman's creativity and frugality (they were made of scraps), they indicate the era's love of rich texture and pattern. Embroidered and painted velvet and silk, crocheted lace. American, c. 1880.

dining room. A center light generally hung over the table, low enough to avoid glaring in the eyes of diners and high enough not to hide people from those opposite them. A dado rail was commonly installed to protect the walls from the chairs (usually placed around the perimeter of the room). Because heavy curtains and hangings were thought to absorb food odors, lightweight fabrics were recommended for dining room windows.

The American kitchen of the late nineteenth century was a private space, devoted to work, and therefore less adorned than the public rooms. But advocates of the attractive kitchen argued that a woman doing her chores in a well-equipped and easily maintained area helped to ensure promptly served meals, a smoothly run household, and a happy, satisfied family. Enamel paint was recommended for wall surfaces because it could be scrubbed when soiled and more easily renewed than wallpaper or wood. Warm grays, creams, Indian reds, and bronze greens were all considered good kitchen colors in the late nineteenth century. Open, painted shelves or cupboards with glass doors were recommended to provide an impetus for keeping the items on the shelves neatly arranged and displayed.

The typical middle-class bedchamber contained a bureau, washstand, table, easy chair, and one or more straight-backed chairs. Bedrooms were not as ornately decorated as dining rooms or parlors, since they were rarely seen by anyone outside the immediate family. Lavish displays of paintings, prints, and bric-a-brac—manifestations of the family's cultural refinement—were unnecessary. The post–Civil War popularization of scientific knowledge about the causes of disease also encouraged simplicity in bedroom furnishings. Physicians urged women to have "sleeping-rooms furnished with rugs instead of carpets, that they may be thoroughly cleaned each week." Carpets were an "evil inasmuch as they absorb impure air, gases, and contagious effluvia, and in the attempt to cleanse them, so much fine dust is thrown into the air."[7] The solution most commonly advocated was the use of "wood carpets,"

65. Much of the intellectual support for the Eastlake Style of furniture came from the drive for a more sanitary environment. Leather seats were easier to clean and did not absorb liquids and dirt. Wood and leather Eastlake Style dining-room chair from a home in Williamsport, Pennsylvania. American, c. 1880–1910.

thin strips of oak which could be covered with easily
cleaned small rugs. Few objects and less ornamentation
eased cleaning and reduced the number of places where
bacteria might flourish. Brass and iron bedsteads were
considered more sanitary than heavy, ornate wooden furniture. For those who preferred bedsteads of mahogany,
oak, cherry, or ash, reformers recommended those with
simple lines, free from elaborate carving (Fig. 66).

Interior decorators who preached sanitation and health
as the key elements in design strongly advised against wallpaper in the bedroom. They thought it harbored the diseases and insect life that the "bad air" of sleeping rooms
fostered. With its "jarring colours and patterns," wallpaper
in bedrooms was "deleterious to bodily health," often leading to a state of "nervous irritability," claimed Robert Edis.
Women were urged to consider the effect the chosen paper
would have on someone confined to the room by illness.

66. This Canadian trade card shows an
"ideal" bedroom. The bedstead is relatively
plain, area or throw rugs are easily picked up
for cleaning, and grooming and cleaning aids
are prominently displayed. Lithographed
trade card. Toronto, Ontario,
c. 1890–1895.

THE TARBOX SHAM HOLDER
PATENTED OCT. 24 1890.
MANUFACTURED BY TARBOX BROS.
TORONTO.

"Everyone," wrote Mary Gay Humphreys, "can . . . recall the restlessness with which a fevered brain will torment itself over set patterns, unreasonable designs, and impossible flowers in wall-paper."[8] For those who persisted in using wallpaper, the message was clear. They were to be very careful in their selection, choosing only those papers with restful, soothing patterns and designs. In spite of the advice of physicians and sanitation reformers, the modestly priced patterned wallpapers of the post–Civil War era continued to be popular among the middle-class.

For Americans of the post–Civil War era, "bathroom" meant a room in which to bathe. The toilet, or water closet, was in a separate room, if in the house at all. During bad weather and at night, families used chamber pots in the house; otherwise a privy in the backyard served as the main toilet. Not until the last decades of the nineteenth century did middle-class Americans begin to think of the bathroom as we know it today—a single room in which tub, sink, and toilet are gathered together.

Unless a house had a "modern" bathroom, most personal hygiene was performed in the bedroom. The washstand with washbowl and pitcher, a sponge, a towel, and a piece of oilcloth for the floor were the usual necessities for thorough bathing. Baths were not an everyday practice. For that occasion, portable tubs of wood, zinc, or painted tin were used, and generally placed in front of a source of heat. By 1900 the separate room for bathing was becoming, as one writer said, "a necessity."[9]

Three types of built-in bathtubs were available by the turn of the century. The best medium-priced tub was elliptically shaped, and made of porcelain-covered iron with a wooden rim around the top which served as a seat. Also in the medium-price range was the painted iron tub on ball-and-claw or, less commonly, paw feet. Solid porcelain tubs were advertised, but their curved top edges were thought to be slippery and unsafe, unlike the wood-rimmed edges of iron tubs.

Nonabsorbent wall surfaces were advised for bathrooms. Glazed ceramic tiles were available in white, buff, and gray, as well as the most desirable but most expensive "tints of roseate sunsets, pearl, and gold."[10] If the expense of fully tiled walls was too great, a dado of tiles was suggested as a compromise. Glass tiles were also available, but less popular. Women were urged to put the decorating money earmarked for the bathroom into tiles rather than any other feature since they were practical and sanitary. If partially tiling the walls was too expensive, paint was the recommended wall treatment. Wallpaper was to be avoided in the bathroom unless varnished, since it was too absorbent. Wood paneling was not recommended either, because, as in the kitchen, it harbored the prolific "water bug," or roach.

Floor coverings were a major concern for a woman decorating a home, particularly if she wanted to reduce the labor required in cleaning carpets. *The Household* suggested that poorer families cover the floors of infrequently used rooms with sized and varnished wallpaper pasted over brown wrapping paper.[11] Oilcloth was a more substantial and popular floor covering for the middle class, and was recommended as a practical solution for covering hall and kitchen floors, which were constantly soiled by the dust and dirt of the unpaved streets and walks. For those who wished higher fashion and less practicality in high-traffic zones, an area rug, rather than carpeting, was recommended.

Many women used carpeting and woven reed or rush matting, either singly or in combination, both to achieve a decorative effect and to extend a carpet's longevity. Often carpeting was recycled by cutting out used sections and either piecing together what was left or buying new borders to enframe the old. In 1882 a subscriber to *The Household* wrote that she had "a Brussels carpet that had been used several years and was too small for the parlor room. But I bought a border for the carpet that made it look 'as good as new' and then got enough colored matting, red & white, to go around the sides of the room, the bordered carpet being put down as a rug in the center of the room." In 1870 Almira MacDonald wrote in her diary that she "made over a carpet of Anns for our front chamber and put it down and put front chamber carpet in my bedroom." In February of the following year she noted: "I had the dining room carpet taken up today and made it over—looks enough better to pay for my trouble." Ten years later, Mrs. MacDonald was still recycling carpet: "Sitting room new carpet laid today and little room upstairs, a carpet made over for it, put down."[12] Frugality and recycling were not simply economic necessities; they were measures of a woman's ability to manage with her family's resources. For the middle class, the cultural values of conspicuous consumption, which served notice of financial and moral success, were counterbalanced by the powerful (also Protestant) concept of virtuous thrift.

In 1883 the *Catalog of the Publications of Louis Prang and Company* criticized the generation of the 1870s because they "thought there could be nothing more beautiful than the representation upon their window drapery of immense tropical jungles of leafage, ferns, and palms, mixed with roses, tulips, and lilies of the valley!" (Fig. 67).[13] By the 1890s this criticism had been embraced by nearly all advisors on domestic fashions. There had been a fashion revolution in window dressing. Light streaming through the large-patterned lace curtains of the 1870s and 1880s was now thought to be garish. Curtains of dotted

67. Elaborate lace curtains were hung inside heavier plush curtains in the parlor. Ivory cotton and floral-pattern lace. American, c. 1870.

muslin, point d'esprit (a delicate, small-patterned lace), and white or cream net with simple patterns inspired by American Indian designs became the favorites of these authors. Muslin was probably the most popular option because it was the easiest to launder and the least expensive to replace when worn or outmoded (Fig. 68). Restraint in decoration became a value for the upwardly mobile and status-conscious elite because the more opulent look had become available to the bulk of the middle class. As in the rectilinear, plain "reform" style furnishings of the Eastlake mode, which had become popular in the 1880s, the canons of simplicity replaced the once-powerful equation of opulence and complexity with wealth and power.

By the 1870s technological innovations in printing and manufacturing reduced the cost of wall decoration—prints, reproductions of academic paintings, photographs, and mirrors. By selecting items which would please the eye, elevate the mind, and evoke appropriate emotional responses, a mother executed her charge to nurture the character of her children. Women who learned about art by visiting the museums and galleries that were thriving in major cities by the end of the nineteenth century, or by reading the reports about artists and their works regularly published by popular magazines, were able to bring art into their home.

In 1883 Louis Prang and Company of Boston offered "facsimiles of oil or water-color paintings by the best artists, in most cases equal to the originals," ranging in price from ten cents for landscapes or floral paintings by minor watercolorists to fifteen dollars for a large *Madonna* after Murillo (Fig. 69). In 1904 Consolidated Portrait and Frame Company of Chicago offered inexpensive frames and five grades of sixteen-by-twenty-inch reproductions, starting at fifteen cents each for their cheapest. They guaranteed them to be of "workmanship good for the price."[14]

Since painting was considered to be one of the finest manifestations of human culture and civilization, it was fitting that the choice and arrangement of artwork in the home be left to women, the "civilizers" of nineteenth-

68. Machine-made muslin curtains, elaborate by twentieth-century standards, were a departure from the naturalistic and complicated designs of the 1880s and 1890s. Muslin curtain with cotton lace inserts. American, c. 1895.

69. Lithographs and photographic reproductions of this and other Madonnas were produced and sold in huge numbers in the latter half of the nineteenth century. They were extremely popular decorations for the parlor. "Madonna della Sedia" (after Raphael), oil on canvas, c. 1880.

century society. Effective execution of this task was another avenue by which women could fulfill their duties of serving their husbands and helping to build their family's reputation. A parlor wall gracefully adorned with a variety of artworks not only displayed the dwellers' erudition and taste, but also evoked the leisured, aristocratic classes to whom fine art had belonged for many centuries. The content of the paintings served as reinforcement of culturally esteemed values, thus aiding in character development and socialization of children. The most popular painting reproductions were those of madonnas painted by Italian Renaissance masters.[15] That revered artists from one of the pinnacles of Western civilization chose motherhood for glorification must have struck a sympathetic chord in nineteenth-century homemakers: they purchased such pictures for their children, husbands, and friends to see and take to heart. Other popular subjects were pastoral landscapes and sublime vistas of American mountains, famous European sights, scenes from classical mythology, and portraits of famous men and current presidents.

While other types of wall decoration may not have carried the status of art reproductions, they echoed the most common themes in painting. Glorification of home or rural life, motherhood, religious themes, and the stages of life also appeared in the needlepoint wall hangings or "mottos" that could be found in nearly every middle-class home. These framed pieces were usually six to eight inches high and ten to fourteen inches wide. Women purchased them with designs already printed on them, and holes punched in the board. By following instructions, either provided with the board or in books and magazines, they could create textile art for their walls.

Family photographs also became popular decorative pieces in the late nineteenth century. Placed on walls and mantels, they reaffirmed the bonds of the family and served as a constant reminder of a family's growth together, from the birth of children to their eventual marriage and departure from the family circle.

Small and large works of art were often densely arranged above the furniture, which was commonly placed against the walls. This achieved a proportional balance in the high-ceilinged rooms of the period. Hanging shelves or wall brackets, on which treasured souvenirs or small sculptures might be perched, were common. So were mirrors. Strategically placed, they could reflect light and wallpaper patterns, and magnify the effect of nearby bric-a-brac.

Sometimes a painting of particular value to the family— a large family portrait, a pleasant landscape, or an inspirational print—would be hung above the piano or parlor organ to create an area ripe for positive familial interaction.[16] The particularly important or favorite work of art could also be highlighted by placing it away from the wall on an easel or pedestal manufactured especially for that purpose.

Pictures chosen for dining rooms not surprisingly offered themes of plenty: still lifes of fruit and other foods were particularly appropriate. Prints and paintings with the theme of hunting, including still lifes of game, were particularly popular at mid-century. As late as the 1880s, Louis Prang and Company offered "Dining-Room Pictures" which included "Dead Game," after G. Bossett, and "Trout" and "Pickerel," after William Harring. Other options were sets of four-color reproductions entitled "Strawberries and Basket," "Cherries and Basket," "Currants," and "Raspberries," after "Miss. Virg. Granberry."

Window shades were used to embellish a room as well as to restrict the amount of light entering it. Available in colored or white holland (a heavy linen or cotton fabric), ticking (a closely woven twill), or tammy cloth (a glazed woolen fabric), some window shades were further ornamented with embroidery, filoselle and crewel, drawnwork borders, lace edges, or stenciled and painted designs (Fig. 70). Portieres—heavy curtains, usually of velvet, brocade, or other rich fabrics—were hung across doorways to retain heat, eliminate drafts, and provide privacy. Sentimental decorative advisors also maintained that they were necessary additions to the Victorian home because "a beautiful room is far more beautiful when there

70. Window shade. Stenciled paper, cotton, and silk. American, c. 1880–1895.

is no square means of egress suggesting the unpleasant idea of departure."[17]

The female realm of decorative textiles covered and softened the usually wooden forms wrought by the male world of machines and commerce. In the household, decoration and decorum—both descendants of the Latin word *decorus,* meaning "beauty"—were the responsibilities of women. The method by which decoration would realize stability was passive and indirect, a dramatic counterpoint to the active and direct means of economic control men exercised in both the outside world and the home. Decoration as moral counterpoint was a viable ideological position and activity so long as ultimate political and economic control resided outside the arena of the decorative—and woman's—realm.

FIVE

H E A L T H
I N B O D Y A N D
M I N D

"The health of the young women of today is of great importance to the nation, for upon their vigor and soundness of body depend to a very great extent the health and capacity of future generations."[1] This warning, by Mary Wood-Allen, chief of the Purity Department of the Woman's Christian Temperance Union, was published in Philadelphia in 1905. In the web of medical theory and cultural analysis of turn-of-the-century America, this seemingly innocuous statement carried a tone of urgency and foreboding for the middle class. Determined to maintain their hegemony as their nation was shaken by labor violence and an unprecedented influx of immigrants, both popular and professional writers—physicians, ministers, and other domestic advisors—tried to isolate and correct the instability and uncertainty that plagued the middle class. They found that the immigrant minority did indeed pose a threat to the social and economic order; but they also located a precipitous decline in the physical and mental fiber of the Anglo-Saxon majority, especially American women.

Publications with detailed information and advice about the health of American women had been popular since the 1840s. Most etiquette or behavior manuals contained at least a chapter on personal care. Catherine Beecher was only one of many commentators and domestic advisors; among the others were Timothy Shay Arthur, Marion Kirkland Reid, J. M. Austin, Josiah Gilbert Holland ("Timothy Titcomb"), Henry Ward Beecher, and Harvey Newcomb.[2] These authors revered "female piety," and concentrated on describing acceptable conventions of social and private behavior. Sexuality was only occasionally discussed, and only in vague, usually metaphorical terms.

The tone and quantity of advice to women about health began to change near the middle of the century. In 1860, in a section entitled "Notes and Queries," the editors of *Godey's* asserted:

It is quite true that prevalent diseases appear to vary with the age we live in. Diphtheria and pneumonia, both so prevalent and fatal the past winter, are strangely suggestive of the hurry of the country, when even Death works more rapidly, and mows down whole ranks of the living. Softening of the brain and insanity are both on the increase; we have it from reliable authority that in England alone, within the last twenty years, insanity has more than tripled. The excitement of life is too stimulating to the brain and nervous powers. . . . "A sober, righteous, and godly life" would seem to be the very best preventive of these new elements of evil; but how hard to pursue it, in the contagion of care, business, and pleasure that meets one at every step.

Three months earlier, in the May 1860 issue of *Godey's*, the editors warned readers not to follow the example of women who had "died of overwork . . . combined with anxiety to excel and please [their] husbands."[3]

By the 1880s the problem of women's health had assumed more dramatic proportions. In *The Household Manual of Domestic Hygiene, Food, and Diet* (1882), J. H. Kellogg, a physician, breakfast cereal magnate, and health food reformer, asserted:

The declining health and strength of American women has come to be a very common observation. Very few young ladies of the present day can compare with their grandmothers of the last generation in powers of physical endurance. Physicians generally acknowledge that at least three-fourths of their practice is derived from diseases of women.

He linked the decline of American women to a variety of causes: "fashionable dress," "sedentary habits," "late hours," "bad diet," "sexual sins," and "too much drugging." By 1887 Kellogg's contention that American women's health was in decline was echoed in the popular women's press. *Demorest's Monthly Magazine,* for example, began a regular column entitled "Sanitarian," which investigated "the care of children . . . [and] how to make our homes healthful through proper drainage and ventilation. We shall look at causes for the alleged early decay of American beauty, and see in what ways it can be arrested."[4]

The intersection—or collision—of health and fashion posed complications for physicians, reformers, and other cultural critics. In a popular publication of 1870, *The Bazar-Book of Decorum*, propriety in table settings and social behavior was accompanied by an aggressively stated critique of the social conceit of deliberate frailty.

> There is a phase of fashion which the doctors might call "morbific," characterized by the affectation of the symptoms of disease. The young Dumas, with his phthisical heroines, as unsound in flesh as in morals, is greatly responsible for the vogue given to the pallid, wan, hectic, and feeble. We thus find the florid and robust assuming ill health when they have it not, and resorting to all kinds of contrivances to give the face a cast of sickliness.
>
> Women are too apt to regard delicacy, in its physical sense of weakness, as an essential element of beauty. This is a false and dangerous notion, which finds expression in the affectation of paleness of complexion and tenuity of figure, which are deliberately acquired by a systematic disobedience of the laws of health. . . . we doubt whether any woman who cultivates sickness and weakness has a sound idea of the value of good looks.

Wanness and fragility as virtues reflect an ideology of deliberate uselessness, and thus a visual identity with those who do not have to work.[5]

The tubercular look alarmed physicians and culture analysts of the 1870s because young women had the obvious responsibility to nurture the next generation, as their forebears had. "Human life," wrote the editors of *The Household*, "is made up of a succession of periods of growth and decay. . . . It should be a great point with all to strive to prolong each period of the ascending series of development, for this would not only prolong life directly, but indirectly, by protracting the descending series of decay. In childhood and in youth particularly, it behooves us to cherish with the utmost care the accumulating fund of vitality."[6] The initial assumption of "periods of growth and decay" equated individual human history with American national history. Historians had demonstrated that empires rose and fell, citing as causes an increase in luxury and a decline in virtue. Aware of this pattern, but armed with the enthusiasm of the Enlightenment, eighteenth-century American leaders had hoped to exempt the nation from this fate. But the promise of the Revolution seemed to have been betrayed by the realities of the century following the signing of the Declaration of Independence. The idea of unbounded individual and social energy was gradually replaced by an assumption of limited growth and possibility. The outcome of the American struggle for existence was no longer a certainty.

Entrusted with the future of the race, women were supposed to be virginal and innocent in their youth, and then they were to become pure and nurturing mothers. Images of ideal women graced the advertising, painting, and public sculpture of the era (Fig. 71). The popular version of the perfect young woman was the girl created by Charles Dana Gibson—long hair generally pinned up, a pure white and unblemished complexion, and complicated drapery on an apparently lush figure (Fig. 72). She was unmistakably upper-middle-class or wealthy.

In their search for the key to women's health, moral and medical reformers became convinced that a woman's general condition was determined by her reproductive system.

> Women's reproductive organs are pre-eminent. They exercise a controlling influence upon her entire system, and entail upon her many painful and dangerous diseases. They are the source of her peculiarities, the center of her sympathies, and the seat of her diseases. Everything that is peculiar to her springs from her sexual organization.[7]

71. The mother figure appeared as Liberty or Columbia throughout the nineteenth century and graced the advertising, painting, and sculpture of the era. "America and Cuba," pencil drawing by Kenyon Cox as study for a magazine cover, c. 1898. (Courtesy Library of Congress.)

Columbia + Cuba – Magazine Cover –
Nude Study

Thus, the time of life when a woman's reproductive system developed was of critical importance. Biological changes in young men clearly produced a physically stronger individual, but the passage to mature womanhood was interpreted as having the opposite effect.[8] According to the prevailing medical theory, the development of the ovaries, uterus, and breasts drained energy from the finite supply each individual possessed. Sexually maturing young

women were therefore cautioned to rest for longer periods of time than in prepuberty years, and to avoid the taxing "brain-work" of education. The popular health writer S. Weir Mitchell, for example, argued that a young woman's "future womanly usefulness was endangered by steady use of her brain." The author of the "Sanitarian" column of *Demorest's Monthly Magazine* similarly warned: "If the health of a girl is sound, the marriageable age should be from twenty to twenty-five or six years. If they have been weakened by overstudy or too much physical labor, the forces should have full time to recover their equilibrium before entering upon this ordeal; for the happiness of families is best secured by the sound health of parents."[9]

Potential dangers to a young woman's maturation into a sexually capable woman were seen everywhere in late-nineteenth-century American society. In this passage from Mary Wood-Allen's *What a Young Woman Ought to*

72. The Gibson style permeated American popular culture. This image of woman was especially prevalent in advertising, and suggests a need to idealize the unblemished White Anglo-Saxon Protestant vision of womanhood. Sketch by Charles Dana Gibson, c. 1895.

Know, the popular connection between novels, sexual development, and nervous disease is clearly articulated:

> I would like to call your attention to the great evil of romance-reading, both in the production of premature development and in the creation of morbid mental states which will tend to the production of physical evils, such as nervous hysteria, and a host of other maladies which depend upon disturbed nerves. Romance-reading by young girls will, by this excitement of the bodily organs, tend to create their premature development, and the child becomes physically a woman months, or even years before she should.

Thirty-five years earlier, in 1870, Orson S. Fowler, a social and architectural critic, also criticized reading material that stimulated the emotions, but he saw more harmful physical side effects.

> Reading of a character to stimulate the emotions and rouse the passions may produce or increase a tendency to uterine congestion, which may in turn give rise to a great variety of maladies, including all the different forms of displacement, the presence of which is indicated by weak backs, painful menstruation and leukorrhea.

In spite of the dire warnings of these guardians of culture and society, such literature continued to be popular.[10]

For the Protestant imagination, pain and suffering were an unavoidable part of life, and they were signals of some sort of justice. Thus, Fowler explained pain in the monthly menstrual cycle as a derivative of "uterine congestion," which in turn was linked to emotions enervated by romantic fiction. Ovulation was a way of "fixing a woman's place in the animal economy. With the act of menstruation is wound up the whole character of her system." Assuming the ideal woman to be free from pain in menstruation, writers throughout the period 1870 to 1910 held to such assertions as: "Whenever there is actual pain at any stage of the monthly period, it is because something is wrong, either in the dress, or the diet, or the personal and social habits of the individual."[11] One ramification of this notion was that the responsibility for painful menstruation was placed squarely on the woman's shoulders. Since it was her fault, her complaints were interpreted as a burden on others. As Almira MacDonald wrote in her diary:

> April 19: I am flowing and have much pain all day— regret to be feeling so miserable for Angus' [her husband's] account.
> April 20: Angus started on the 9:40 train for Chicago. Feeling better. So hard to have him go when not well, from me, but must hope for the best.[12]

Light housework was commonly—and conveniently—recommended as the best way to regulate the menses and decrease the pain. Study and reading, however, allegedly drew too much energy and blood from the genital area, thereby further weakening the sufferer and potentially damaging her reproductive system.[13]

Menopause, rather than being considered a liberation from the "peculiarity" and inconvenience of menstruation, was characterized as a transition to be feared. Commenting on activities during puberty and their link to menopause, author and physician Emma Drake maintained: "Just here many of the seeds are sown that bring forth a harvest of diseases in the following years, and many things that have been laid to our ancestors remotely distant are really the result of wrong-doing and living in the first decade and a half of our lives."[14] That is, early "sins" may seem undetected and unpunished, but time will inevitably bring painful retribution. Presenting menopause as a traumatic change served a number of purposes. Physicians and domestic advisors used this threat of future trauma to argue against "sexual indulgence," fashionable lifestyles, and women's suffrage.

The genital theory of female health meant that women were expected to be ill because they were women. While such a theory was crudely self-serving for the male populace (who labored under no such burden), it was also indicative of more subtle and elusive cultural concerns. The continual assertion of feminine inferiority, both mental and physical, perhaps suggests a fear of women's power as the carriers and supporters of infant life, and hence the race. The uterus was a fertile place with life-giving and life-sustaining potential, but Western civilization had been simultaneously possessed by awe and fear of dark, warm, and enclosed places for centuries: the uterus was both the genesis of life and the heart of darkness.[15]

Literature might excite the passions, and study might harm women's nervous and reproductive systems, but clothing fashions, and especially corsets, were thought to cause direct physical damage. Made of coarse cotton or buckram, with stiff supporting wires and steel bands, corsets tightly laced a woman's waist, so that she appeared several inches smaller than she was (Fig. 73). The list of maladies attributed to, or in some way linked to, corseting included broken ribs, collapsed lungs, weakening of abdominal walls (therefore necessitating the use of forceps when delivering a baby), neurasthenia, and an inverted or prolapsed uterus. *The Bazar-Book of Decorum* (1870) compared corseting to the ancient Chinese custom of footbinding: "The process of our dames hardly differs from that of the Chinese women, whose feet, from the early age of five years, are so firmly bandaged, that, as they say themselves, they become dead."[16]

Critics of corsets, or "tight lacing," were numerous throughout the nineteenth century. In 1846 Orson Fowler attacked the use of the corset in a book whose title reveals most of his argument: *Tight-Lacing, Founded on Physiology and Phrenology; or, the Evils Inflicted on the Mind and Body by Compressing the Organs of Animal Life, Thereby Retarding and Enfeebling the Vital Functions.* Fowler based his attack on the assumption that "compression of any part produced inflammation." As a consequence of compression, according to Fowler, blood would flow to the woman's head, thereby putting pressure on her

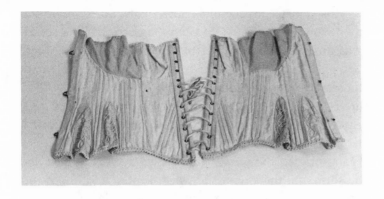

73. The laces of the corset were the key to its adjustability, and hence to the degree to which women could mold their figures. Bone structure prevented too much constriction around the hips, but the midriff could be subjected to severe tightening. Cotton corset. American, c. 1860–1900.

nervous system, which would cause a personality change. Even more ominous to most Americans was his second assertion: blood which was restricted in its flow to and from the lower regions of the body would also cause inflammation, and this compression of the "lower organs" would serve to excite "amative desires." Thus, when women chose the corset, they not only sacrificed their bodies and nerves for fashion, but also endangered their morality and the morality of the men around them. The responsibility for male sexual aggression therefore could be linked to a woman's choice of fashion (Fig. 74).[17]

74. Trade sign for Warner's corsets. Lithographed cardboard. American, c. 1910.

Most nineteenth-century critics of the corset, whether they were feminists or physicians, agreed that the corset was an evil, but for different reasons. Physicians seized upon the idea that corsets compressed the genitals and thereby weakened a woman's ability to bear healthy children. The irony of this was that the corset damaged precisely what it was supposed to enhance. Corsets distorted women's bodies to stress their procreative functions. Tight-lacing pushed the breasts up and enlarged them visually by shrinking the size of the waist. Bustles and hoops for skirts (Fig. 75), usually of wood, metal, or bone, gave the illusion of an enlarged pelvis and the subliminal promise of sexuality, fecundity, and easy delivery.[18]

Physicians summoned the power of traditional and contemporary scientific theory in their argument that the promising maternal capabilities of the corset, skirts, and bustle were not only a sham, but also dangerous to the future of the race. Utilizing first the Lamarckian assertion that artificially acquired physical characteristics could be transmitted to future generations, they maintained that corseting had gradually narrowed women's pelvic regions. Then, employing Darwin's popular and powerful theory of natural selection, they warned that these slim-hipped women would tend to produce children with smaller and smaller heads. Such a trend was dangerous, they argued, because Western civilization needed more and more "head-workers." They discounted forceps delivery because it had allowed women with small pelvises to successfully bear children, hence passing on their diminished pelvic size to their daughters.[19]

The corset could also cause a prolapsed, or sagging, uterus. Physicians alleged that it was possible for the uterus to invert and protrude from the vagina. Remedies for the prolapsed uterus included sponges forced into the vagina, injections of alum and water, the application of faradic electricity (which was thought to strengthen abdominal muscles), tonics, enemas, hip baths, and pessaries (uterine supports).[20]

Pessaries were patented and sold in a variety of forms

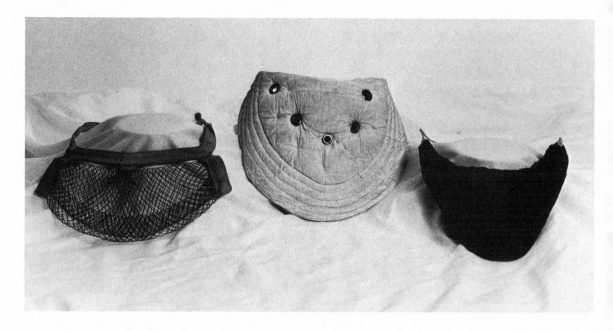

and materials; between 1850 and 1885, at least twenty-six were patented. There were seven basic types of pessary, made of wood, bone, metal, or combinations thereof. One of the most common forms consisted of a slightly hollowed-out, rounded disk of metal, India rubber, or ivory, which was connected to a cylindrical stem (Fig. 76). A spring mechanism inside the stem or a simple band of spring steel exerted the upward pressure on the uterus once the mechanism was inserted in the vagina. A steel wire continued vertically along the exterior of the abdomen,

75. Bustles were attached by means of hooks or laces to the waistband, which also held the petticoats. Along with the corset, the bustle created a caricature image of a woman's body. Steel and cotton bustle pads.
American, c. 1835–1840.

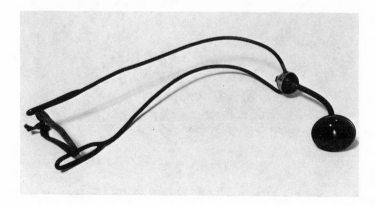

76. To counteract the effects of corsets, which often caused prolapse of the uterus, uterine support devices called pessaries appeared in a wide variety of forms. Cup pessary with rubber cup, steel rods, and elastic waistband.
Patent model, 1871.

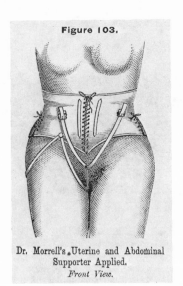

Dr. Morrell's Uterine and Abdominal
Supporter Applied.
Front View.

77. The trade catalog of the Shepard and
Dudley Manufacturing Company illustrated
the use of Dr. Morrell's uterine and
abdominal supporter. New York, c. 1870.

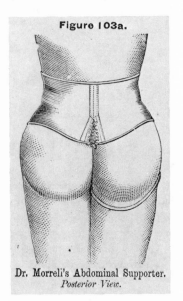

Dr. Morrell's Abdominal Supporter.
Posterior View.

where it was connected to a waistband (Fig. 77). Another popular form was the ring pessary, generally made of hard rubber, and also attached to a waistband (Fig. 78). The wing pessary, with ivory, wood, or rubber wings, was inserted and the stem turned to open the wings (Fig. 79 and 80). The pelvic pessary, so called because of its resemblance to the pelvic bone, was designed to support the uterine neck, and therefore prevent or cure a prolapsed uterus (Fig. 81). This particular form was available in different sizes, with the advantage that it did "not interfere with the act of coition." The spiral spring pessary included a spring-loaded rubber cup to support the uterus; this mechanism was attached to a cloth or elastic belt worn around the waist (Fig. 82). Women were advised to remove this and nearly all other types of pessary when they retired for the night (the obvious exceptions were those worn entirely within their bodies). The pessary could then be reinserted "and readjusted before assuming an erect position in the morning."[21]

Feminists attacked corseting because of its potential harm to internal organs and its obvious restriction of movement. In *Dress-Reform*, a collection of five essays by women (four of whom were physicians) published in 1874,

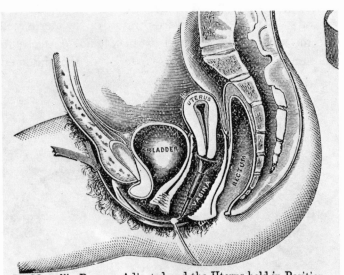

Dr. Morrell's Pessary Adjusted and the Uterus held in Position.

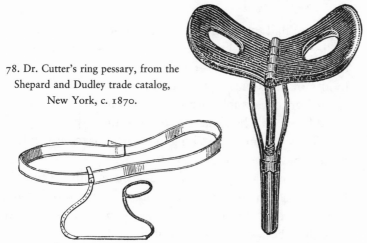

78. Dr. Cutter's ring pessary, from the Shepard and Dudley trade catalog, New York, c. 1870.

79. Modification of Zwang's pessary, from the Shepard and Dudley trade catalog, New York, c. 1870.

80. This pessary combined aspects of the wing and cup designs. Once the device was inserted, the stem was turned, thereby opening up the wings to reveal the rubber cup. Patent model, 1877.

fashion was characterized as a "despotic gooddess" and a "juggernaut." In her essay on female anatomy, Carolyn Hastings portrayed the corset as an "instrument of human torture," and linked it to malfunctions of the reproductive, digestive, and respiratory systems. The authors agreed that "what is needed, then, is not to assail fashion, but to teach hygiene—to awaken women to a consciousness of the injuries that follow the wearing of their present garments, and to demonstrate that it is in their power so to modify this tight, heavy, and complicated style of apparel as to increase the strength, ability, and happiness of themselves and of their children." The lessons of the immediate past had made it clear that a new tactic was in order.

It was supposed that from bad clothes to good was but a step, and that the only preliminaries necessary were to devise the best possible apparel and to invite everyone to adopt it. The most notable of these failures was the Bloomer costume. . . . It was, indeed, true that many had grown restless under the burdens and restrictions of their dress. . . . But to the majority of thoughtless women it remained an object of indifference or of ridicule.

The essayists called on physicians to exercise their influence over women's attire. During the nineteenth century, the

81. Pelvic pessaries were worn wholly internally, and had the advantage of not disrupting sexual intercourse. Although women were urged to remove pessaries upon retiring, it is not clear that they did so. Painted wood patent models, 1877.

82. Attached to a waistband like the cup and wing pessaries, the spring pessary utilized a relatively recent development of the late nineteenth century, spring steel, to provide support. Steel and rubber patent model, 1867.

physician had taken on some of the moral responsibilities earlier centuries had reserved for the minister, or even the family. Thus, the dress-reformers maintained that "all modes of dress that injure the human body, or make the wearer uncomfortable, are strictly within the province of the doctor; and he should never lose the opportunity to benefit his patients by teaching them the evils to be avoided by sensible reform of dress."[22]

The changes sought by reformers began with the corset. In an 1874 issue of *The Household*, one columnist laconically stated: "That our dress may be more healthful, it must first be made looser about the waist, as loose as a man's." Another writer, known as "Aida," wrote five years later:

> I omitted corsets when speaking of underthings. They have been banished from my wardrobe so long I had almost forgotten there was such an article. . . . There has been so much written against corsets that it doesn't seem as if there was need of more words on the subject. . . . One feels so perfectly free and easy, especially if you wish to make any distance you will notice a difference. . . . But I shouldn't advise you when you leave off your corsets to put [on] a pair of old-fashioned "stays" full of whalebones and laced as tightly as you wear your corsets.

One of the secondary hazards of corsets was that they provided a mechanism whereby skirts could be supported from the waist. Such a system, as Abba Gould Woolson pointed out, "encased the thoracic region" with "from six to ten thicknesses" of fabric in the form of skirts, which in turn were supported by bustles and hoops. This weight suspended from the waist and hips allegedly displaced and distorted internal organs, adding to the deformities created by the compression of the corset.[23]

Aware that the bloomer-type costume had "gained but little favor," reformers advocated underwear that united the vest and lower garment, thereby suspending most of the weight from the shoulders. They also urged women to wear wool stockings and "leggins" in winter, and flannel or "union" undergarments, rather than "the thick quilted and wadded ones our grandmothers wore." This arrangement would more uniformly protect women from cold, rather than the fashionable system in which "the lower extremities are covered . . . with but one thickness, and that of cotton. Under such circumstances, an effort to obtain proper warmth is usually made by adding an extra supply of skirts."[24]

Winter petticoats and skirts, which could weigh as much as thirty pounds, were hung from a compressed waist and supported by feet on high-heeled shoes. Popular women's shoes in the late nineteenth century were commonly of leather, with leather soles and heels. While such shoes usually had uppers that were laced or buttoned to the bottom of the calf, they nonetheless were unstable because of slick soles and high heels. Moreover, it was fashionable to have small or dainty feet, and fashion-conscious women often wore shoes too narrow or too short for their feet. Standardized shoe sizes were introduced before the Civil War, and became common by the 1880s. The mechanization and standardization of the human foot into numbered sizes had a fashionable ramification beyond presenting evidence of the broader cultural trend toward standardization. If smallness was considered a virtue, then progressively numbered foot sizes (with higher numbers equaling larger feet) gave women and men comparative, measurable data upon which to pass judgment on women's bodies.

Physicians and dress-reformers vehemently attacked the fashion of high-heeled shoes. Woolson argued:

The Chinese shock our moral sense when they deform the feet of their women by merciless compression in infancy; . . . the high heels which had been so fashionable, but which are now, happily, less used, are one of the most fruitful sources of disease. They not only cause contractions of the muscles of the legs . . . [but also] induce the corns and bunions that alone suffice to make locomotion very painful.

In 1870 *Godey's* ran a column by their contributing physician, Dr. Charles P. Uhle, who warned against "tight-fitting" shoes and advised soaking to relieve the pain.[25]

There were different approaches among dress-reformers anxious to convince women to give up the high heel. One of *The Household*'s contributing authors measured the progress that had been made already: "A century and a half ago . . . our grandmothers in Europe [wore] the French heel on their boots three inches in height, which is more than the French heel of today. . . . You can get sensible shoes now if you want them." Dr. John H. Kellogg, writing in 1883, expressed no such optimism. He stated that the "stiff, unnatural, mincing gait of the fashionable young lady is not so much an affectation as a necessity with her." The shoes that have survived from the era and advertisements in such mass-market publications as the *Sears Roebuck Catalog* seem to support Kellogg's version of the footwear preferences of the middle-class woman (Fig. 83).[26]

In spite of dire warnings, corsets and high-heeled shoes remained extremely popular throughout the late nineteenth century, as the fashion plates published in women's magazines demonstrate (Fig. 84 and 85). The tenacity of this fashion is attributable to an entire ideology of womanhood, rather than simply to women's preferences in

83. High heels provoked an outcry among both men and women concerned with feminine health. Women's shoes, leather and cotton cord. American, c. 1890.

84. Advertising poster for *Frank Leslie's Illustrated Magazine*, New York, c. 1870.

85. Women's clothing was extremely complex and restrictive. Imagine ironing these dresses! Fashion plate, *Godey's Lady's Book,* June 1880.

dress. In his "Economic Theory of Women's Dress" (1894), Thorstein Veblen incisively and convincingly presented the corseted woman's inability to move easily as evidence of her role as an object signifying her husband's wealth and power. Single women indicated that they were potentially suitable ornaments, with all the procreative possibilities of an enlarged bosom and pelvis.[27]

Corsets did indicate at least the guise of wealth for would-be aristocratic women, as well as the status aspirations of their husbands. Since corsets made bending, stooping, and picking up extremely difficult, women who wore them were suggesting that they had others employed to perform these functions. Corsets had been fashionable in aristocratic European settings of the seventeenth and eighteenth centuries, and wearing this gear was part of the middle-class American attempt to duplicate the courtly traditions of the Continent. Other material manifestations of their popular enthusiasm for the courts of the crowned heads of Europe were the furniture styles named for the French kings, as well as the curvilinear rococo and blockier "Renaissance" forms manufactured during the latter half of the nineteenth century.[28]

These clothing and furniture fashions were for the public sphere, and they were most appropriately worn and displayed outside the house or in the rooms of the house devoted to the rituals of communication and show. In a densely furnished parlor or dining room, women presented themselves to emissaries from the outside who were of sufficient status to pass through the hallway and into the parlor. Restricted movement was almost a requirement because the room was so crowded with furnishings. The parlor was the ultimate middle-class arena for display of wealth and power in an age when more elaborate goods and fashions were available to the middle class than ever before.[29]

The fashionable display of womanhood in these circumstances was condemned for medical reasons, but in effect concurred with the critics' ideological positions on sexuality. The purity literature of the period—etiquette books, religious tracts, medical articles, and hygiene manuals—depicted sex as the basest of human drives, in stark contrast to the manuals of the seventeenth and eighteenth centuries, in which pleasure was considered a normal and necessary part of the act of coition. Aberrant behavior inevitably would be detected (one showed signs) and severely punished by disease or mental anguish. Clerics and physicians used a variety of tactics, including phrenology, to threaten and cajole potentially active women and men.[30]

Marion Harland, author of *Eve's Daughter; or, Common Sense for the Maid, Wife, and Mother* (1882), and Emma Drake, who wrote *What a Young Wife Ought to Know* (1908), were ministers' wives who advocated marital continence; sexual intercourse was primarily for the purpose of procreation. Like most marriage-manual writers, they asserted that infrequent intercourse was a sign of civilization, elevating white (and presumably Protestant) people above others genetically and evolutionarily inferior. Purity writers also held that continence would help decrease the power of sexuality, thus liberating women to wear more comfortable and practical clothing (i.e., shorter skirts) "without the sensuous desires of men being aroused," as Delos Wilcox put it. Mary Wood-Allen urged women to have "comparatively little sexual passion," and to touch their husbands "without a particle of sexual desire."[31]

The catalog of forbidden sexual acts included orgasm ("voluptuous spasms"), which was thought to interfere with conception and even cause sterility, as well as masturbation, the "solitary vice." Women were warned:

> The results of self-abuse are most disastrous. It destroys mental power and memory, it blotches the complexion, dulls the eye, takes away strength, and may even cause insanity. It is a habit most difficult to overcome, and may, not only last for years, but its tendency may be transmitted to one's children . . . no habit is more tyrannical than the dominion of unrestrained sexual desire.

Others would be informed of the woman's vice by her indolence, pale cheeks, tenderness of the spine, backaches, nervousness, "peevishness," irritability, moroseness, disobedience, and "unnatural appetites for mustard, pepper, cloves, clay, and salt."[32]

Marital continence and the prohibition of masturbation were defended as part of a general ideology of white racial superiority. For men, release of seminal fluid was thought to weaken them physically and prevent maximum intellectual development. By practicing continence, argued Emma Drake, sperm would be reabsorbed in the bloodstream, and assimilated by the brain. Drake was echoing a long-held belief in the potency of human sperm. Sylvester Graham—grain miller, food faddist, and social critic—wrote in the late 1830s that American men were suffering from an increased incidence of skin diseases, nervousness, and headaches. He posited that semen and blood were produced in a one-to-forty ratio, and concluded that American men were suffering because they were too active sexually. He advocated that men restrict intercourse to twelve times per year, and that they change their diet to include more grains, and especially more Graham flours.[33]

The practical material response advocated by purity crusaders was twin beds for married couples.

> It is considered far more healthful for grown people to occupy different beds. The air which surrounds the body under the bed clothing is exceedingly impure, being impregnated with the poisonous substances which have escaped through the pores of the skin. Celebrated physicians have condemned the double bed.[34]

In spite of pronouncements by "celebrated physicians" and marriage-manual authors, the double bed endured as the most common bedroom furniture form in America. Nineteenth-century catalogs of furniture manufacturers and mass-marketing firms contain almost no examples of twin beds.[35]

Though women were encouraged to be uninterested in sex, an occasional critic, such as Elizabeth Blackwell, pointed out that a woman's repugnance toward sex was probably a response to fears of pain, injury (if not death) in childbirth, and past experiences with brutal or awkward partners.[36] In this sense, prevailing public attitudes concerning sexuality, which twentieth-century analysts have labeled "Victorian prudery," perhaps reflected a need for women to maintain some sort of dignity in a legal and physical relationship in which they were subordinate. This denial of sex and self ironically gave women a modicum of dignity and power.

The characterization of sex as base and animalistic was consistent with late-nineteenth-century concepts of women's bodily health. Cleanliness and order were moral imperatives, both in the physical space of the home and in the appearance of a woman. Discussion of a woman's body and her house are almost interchangeable.

Personal cleanliness—maintaining "the house of her soul"—was paramount. In the bedroom this meant "no uncovered vessel, no old shoes in the closet, no soiled underclothing"; all were considered dangerous because they gave off "impure vapors."[37] This idea, reminiscent of medieval fears of the vapors that were thought to generate spontaneously in prisons and dungeons, was modified and modernized by popular interpretations of Pasteur's discovery that micro-organisms transmitted disease.[38] Bedrooms were considered particularly dangerous sources of potential disease because of American sleeping and washing practices. *The Household* stated: "Neither the unhealthful thing called a comfortable nor the unsightly covering known as a patched quilt should be seen in a bed on this day." Dr. E. G. Cook wrote in *Demorest's Monthly Magazine:*

> Every sleeping room should have outside windows, opening at the top and bottom, and sunshine at some part of the day. . . . It would be better for people to live in tents the whole year round than in some of the damp, dark places in which they are huddled in our cities, where are no possibilities for cleanliness or pure air.

Cook argued that "about forty per cent of all deaths are due to the influence of impure air."[39]

An even more alarmist statistic on the link between poor ventilation and poor health was offered in the August 1889 issue of *Good Housekeeping*. The article, entitled "Air-Famine," cited a physician's discovery that "55 out of 100 white children die before they complete seven years of life . . . hardly five of that number are born with germs of an early death . . . two thirds of the remainder perish from want of life-air." *The Household* ran an extended series in 1889, "The Art of Preserving Health," which began with columns discussing the importance of pure air. *Godey's* had similarly issued a manifesto, "Fifteen Rules for the Preservation of Health," in 1860. Rule number one mandated fresh air; other rules urged moderation in eating, forbade "strong drinks, tobacco, snuff, and opium," and advocated exercise, sunlight, and cleanliness in the home.[40]

According to *The Bazar-Book of Decorum* (1870), "daily bathing in cold water" was a "main requisite for giving health, strength and grace to the human body." *The Household* advised women that "no matter how humble your room may be, there are eight things it should contain: a mirror, washstand, soap, towel, comb, hair brush, nail-brush, and tooth-brush." These were usually accompanied by a pitcher and basin. As Mary Wood-Allen remarked:

> Bathing appliances are marks of civilization, and the bath-room is becoming a necessity. Where the bathroom does not exist it is easy to bathe thoroughly and completely. A wash-basin of water, with a sponge and a towel, furnish all that is absolutely necessary. . . . nothing is so efficient a protection from the cold as a foot-bath.

Good "housekeeping" for the body meant interior cleanliness as well. According to Wood-Allen, "Many girls feel that it is more delicate to neglect the care of the bowels than to attend to a daily evacuation . . . it is only politeness and refinement to see that this part of their bodily housekeeping is daily attended to."[41]

Cooking techniques, eating habits, and kitchen cleanliness were critically important because the "fuel" for the "living engine" was prepared there. As Dr. E. G. Cook phrased it in the September 1887 issue of *Demorest's*: "There can be no more important subject. The stomach is the center of life." A more strident equation had been made by Dr. J. H. Kellogg in 1876: "Men and women are subject to few diseases whose origin may not be traced to the kitchen. Closely following diseased physical natures come mental and moral inefficiency originating in the same prolific cause."[42]

"Good blood" was a result of "good digestion," which in turn required "good teeth" and "good food." Failure at any point in the process would lead to the "American disease," dyspepsia, or chronic indigestion. *Godey's* proclaimed, that "the prevalence of dyspepsia in Americans is simply the result of a century of bad cookery. . . . More especially women have suffered. Having little opportunity for exercise, much confined at home . . . women as a class are the victims of chronic dyspepsia." Dr. Cook contended that "dyspepsia—for which this nation is famed—would shortly disappear if people could be induced to eat the right kind of food, and only enough of it to keep the balance of waste and supply."[43] In the same way that male drunkenness had been blamed on women's "failures" in the maintenance of neat and pleasant homes, overindulgent eating of greasy and highly seasoned foods was the fault of the "mistress of the kitchen." Thus the "American disease" was a woman's problem; men were acquitted of responsibility for their own choices. Women found themselves in the unenviable position of apparently having two "centers" of their lives. If cookery and digestion were so important, why did so many physicians trace mental and physical maladies to the reproductive system?

For many post-war reformers, exercise was a cure-all for the various ills of modern life, such as corsets, "French heels," inadequate diet, and airlessness. Only in combination with the encouragement of outdoor exercise and physical activity were critics able to effect some alteration in dress. Perhaps more than anything else, the "bicycle craze" of the 1880s doomed the corset.

The temple of the body was only as good as the temple of the mind, and the mind, too, showed foreboding signs of decay and weakness in the latter half of the nineteenth century. In 1860 the editors of *Godey's* had linked insanity and "softening of the brain" to "the excitement of life." The "excitement" was a result of the increased prosperity of the new urban industrial culture of America. This bureaucratic economic structure needed a labor force that worked not with their hands as their agrarian ancestors had, but with their brains. The price of this new order was a new malady—neurasthenia. In *American Nervousness: Its Causes and Consequences* (1881), George Beard contended that neurasthenia was an indicator of an advanced cultural level, and therefore not necessarily evil.

Although the disease could lead to insanity, it was possible to treat it, once sufferers understood its causes. Beard linked neurasthenia to Protestant culture, maintaining that Roman Catholic cultures were free from it because they lacked individualism, intellectual challenges, and social intercourse. Black Americans and American Indians were similarly unaffected; Beard characterized them as children "who have never matured in the higher ranges of intellect," and who were "living not for science or ideas, but for the senses and emotions."[44]

The disease was also absent from the farm. Neurasthenia was an urban phenomenon. According to Beard, "As would logically be expected, neurasthenia is oftener met with in cities than in the country, is more marked and more frequent at the desk, the pulpit, and the counting-room than in the shop or on the farm."[45]

The symptoms were many: sensitivity to weather changes, insomnia, depression, dyspepsia, spermatorrhea, timidity, tenderness in the scalp, teeth, or gums, abnormal secretions, itching, flushing, "fidgetiness," pulse palpitations, headaches, chills, heat flashes, "morbid" fears, dilated pupils, sweaty hands, writer's cramps, dry skin, yawning, and hopelessness. Neurasthenia was not a single disease as twentieth-century medical theory defines it; it was as much ideology as malady.[46]

The pulpit, counting house, and desk were male areas of work. For urban men, neurasthenia was equal to a superior mind, and indicated that the Protestant part of the white race was moving up the evolutionary ladder. A measure of the ideological content of Beard's conception of the disease is that he did not regard women sufferers with the same approval. In *Eating and Drinking: A Popular Manual of Food and Diet on Health and Disease* (1871), Beard asserted that women used their brains "little and on trivial matters," and that a woman's cranial capacity was ninety percent of that of the male. Other physicians agreed. In 1889 Dr. Arabella Kenealy argued that listlessness rather than intellectual work was the cause of the urban woman's neurasthenia. She maintained that when middle-class women were relieved of their chores by household conveniences, they became bored. She urged such women to discover their "nobler sphere," which, according to ideological dictates, was paradoxically in the home. The way back to mental health was through domesticity: baking bread, canning fruits, and home economy.[47]

Beginning with an assumption of mental and physical inferiority, physicians and authors of behavior manuals argued that activity in the business world would generate and further aggravate a female neurasthenic's condition. Physician Moses T. Runnells posited that professional women gradually lost interest in childbearing, and noted that educated women wanted to decrease the number of children they bore.[48] According to such medical practitioners as Beard, Runnells, and Kenealy, the ironic outcome of this disease of an advanced industrial society was that white Anglo-Saxon Protestant Americans would have fewer children, while the "lower races" of working-class immigrants and Roman Catholics would grow in number, and ultimately claim the power and influence of the established elite.

If individuals possessed a finite amount of nervous energy, and "brain-work" required more of it, then help for neurasthenics logically centered on rest and the control of emotions which might further drain a woman's nervous energy. Women were urged to get fresh air, avoid excitement and sexual activity, and to refrain from taking too much tea, playing cards, and engaging in excessive mental labor when young.[49] The message was clear and full of foreboding. Only if women refrained from those activities which might challenge the role of men in the power structure of the nation would they be able to fulfill the destiny and promise of America. Once afflicted with professional aspirations or neurasthenia, women who lost interest in sexual intercourse and procreation (theoretically its only legitimate end) were urged to forgo sex to become healthy enough to procreate properly.

Low-voltage electricity was one of the most popular

cures for neurasthenia. Physicians compared the human nervous system to a galvanic battery, and posited that certain seasons (autumn and winter) and certain hours of the day (9 A.M. to noon, 6 to 9 P.M.) were high in positive energy, and therefore nervous individuals were most active at those times.[50] One of the most revealing texts on the electrical treatment of neurasthenia is *A Practical Treatise on the Medical and Surgical Uses of Electricity Including Localized and General Electricalization* (1871), by Alphonso D. Rockwell and George Beard. This *Treatise* appeared in a multitude of popular forms (Fig. 87), es-

86. Electricity was one of the great popular innovations of turn-of-the-century America. Its powers were mysterious but potent for the popular imagination. It was considered, as the handle of this brush reminds us, "the germ of all life." Advertisement from *Harper's Weekly*, October 29, 1881.

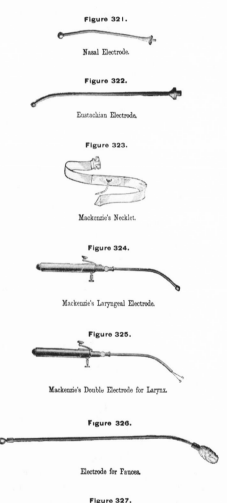

Figure 321.

Nasal Electrode.

Figure 322.

Eustachian Electrode.

Figure 323.

Mackenzie's Necklet.

Figure 324.

Mackenzie's Laryngeal Electrode.

Figure 325.

Mackenzie's Double Electrode for Larynx.

Figure 326.

Electrode for Fauces.

Figure 327.

Dental Electrode, insulated in different styles.

pecially in advertisements in such women's monthly magazines as *Godey's* and *Demorest's,* and in *Harper's Weekly* (Fig. 86). The symptoms cured were usually roughly equivalent to the extended list of symptoms of neurasthenia. The trade catalog of the New York firm of Shepard and Dudley from about 1880 illustrates four types of galvanic batteries available to physicians, and forty-four different electrodes, to be applied on or inside various parts of the body.[51]

Tonics, elixirs, and other patent medicines were also widely prescribed for treating neurasthenia. The most common element in these potions was alcohol. "Baker's Stomach Bitters," for example, was 42.6 percent alcohol; "Warners Safe Tonic Bitters" was 35.7 percent; and two of the most popular brands, "Lydia Pinkhams's Vegetable Compound" (Fig. 88) and "Ayer's Sarsaparella," were 20.6 and 26.2 percent alcohol. Pharmacies in the late nineteenth century often dispensed liquid cures by the dose, accompanied by bromides or soda water.[52]

Paregoric (camphorated tincture of opium), "Dover's Powder" (ipecac and opium), and laudanum (tincture of opium) were the most common forms of opium available to consumers in the late nineteenth century (Fig. 89). Opium imports had steadily increased throughout the middle of the nineteenth century—from 24,000 pounds in 1840 to 416,824 pounds in 1872—and, according to state-commissioned reports published between 1872 and 1900, women were the primary users of the drug. This evidence of addiction to "tonics" was, for physicians and other analysts, an affirmation of their initial assumption of women's weakness and inferiority.[53]

Crusaders against alcohol joined the medical profession in condemning patent medicines and the women who used them. Dr. J. H. Kellogg asserted:

Bitters are filthy compounds of various nauseous drugs and poisons and bad whiskeys. *All* of them contain alcohol. "Temperance Bitters" and "Vinegar Bitters" are no exceptions. Some contain more alcohol and fusel-oil than do brandy, gin, or rum. The various "blood tonics," "purifiers," "invigorators," etc. are of the same character. Their manufacturers are deserving of a place in the deepest part of the bottomless pit.[54]

By 1905 the temperance advocates' critique of patent medicines and the characterization of neurasthenia as a women's disease were linked in a direct way. Mary Wood-Allen argued that "much of the neurasthenia . . . now so common in that portion of the female sex who have ample means and leisure to indulge in any luxury agreeable to their taste . . . is due to narcotics."[55] The circle was complete. What began as a disease of the urban "brain-worker," who occupied his place in the advanced corporate, urban world because he had evolved to a higher, more sophisticated form of life, was transformed into a disease of indolent women of leisure. Formerly treated with a variety of drugs, electricity, and alcoholic patent medicines, it was by 1905 thought to be the effect of such compounds.

Hysteria was the other major new disease of the late nineteenth century. Dr. Charles P. Uhle described the symptoms, causes, and care of the disease in an extensive article in *Godey's* in 1870:

A hysterical woman is a pitiful and unfortunate object—full of aches and pains, and imaginary ills, capricious in character, whimsical in conduct, excitable, impatient, obstinate, and frivolous—a regular Gordian knot for friends and physicians to unravel. She possesses a most variable and imaginative disposition, which, in spite of all that can be done, keeps her in a continued whirl of excitement from morning until night.

The article described the classic symptoms of paranoia ("she conceives an idea that poison has been mixed with her food") and manic depression ("A word will make her laugh or cry, and the merest trifles will make her transcendently happy, or cast her into gloomy despair").

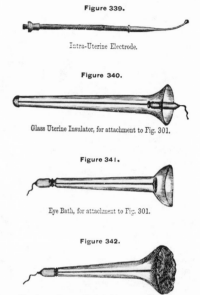

Figure 339.

Intra-Uterine Electrode.

Figure 340.

Glass Uterine Insulator, for attachment to Fig. 301.

Figure 341.

Eye Bath, for attachment to Fig. 301.

Figure 342.

Sponge Glass, for attachment to Davis & Kidder's Electro Magnetic Machine

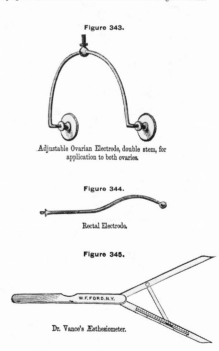

Figure 343.

Adjustable Ovarian Electrode, double stem, for application to both ovaries.

Figure 344.

Rectal Electrode.

Figure 345.

W.F.FORD,N.Y.

Dr. Vance's Æsthesiometer.

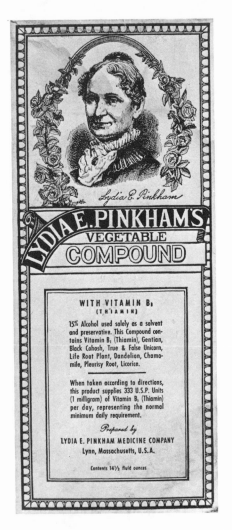

88. "Lydia Pinkham's," probably the most famous of all the patent medicines, was advertised in nearly every issue of such popular magazines as *Godey's* and *Peterson's*. It contained fifteen percent alcohol "as a solvent and preservative." Bottle for Lydia E. Pinkham's Vegetable Compound, Lynn, Massachusetts, c. 1920.

In case of an accident, a fire, a sudden surprise or fright, or even a disappointment, a denial, or a cross word . . . she goes into convulsions or fits, . . . she shrieks, and screams, and tears her hair; she bites herself and others; she throws her limbs convulsively about, twists her body in all kinds of violent contortions; trembles, sweats, and gasps for breath; beats her breast with her clenched fists; groans, weeps, and not unfrequently requires the assistance of others to keep her from doing herself irreparable injury.

Hysteria was a women's disease. Although the manifestations of hysteria resembled those of insanity, physicians were careful to distinguish between hysteria and the condition of a "raving maniac." Implicit in the popular and professional literature on hysteria and insanity are distinctions of class: hysteria was usually, though not always, linked with middle-class and wealthy women; "mania" with the poor.[56]

The causes of hysteria, like the causes of neurasthenia, were often confused with symptoms, and Uhle pointed out that "it is but poorly understood." Suggested causes included "weak constitution, scrofula, indolence, a city life, bad physical and moral education, nervous or sanguine temperaments; the over excitement of certain feelings, and religious or other enthusiasm."[57] This curious combination of environmentalism, heredity, and other communicable diseases as causes for hysteria implicitly demonstrates that physicians and the popular media chose to isolate hysteria as a social malady, connected to the role of middle-class and wealthy women in the culture of the American city. This was a disease of women only; the root of the word is the Greek *hystera,* or womb.

Prevention of hysteria and care for the hysterical woman took two forms. Uhle advised friends and physicians to "indulge her on her whims and caprices, . . . sympathize with her on her *troubles,* for it should be recollected that her fanciful notions are *realities* to her." For medication, "the tonic plan of treatment" is recommended, especially those potions "which have a special tendency to the nervous system." Other treatments to prevent "paroxysms" included

> the daily use of the cold bath, exercise in the open air, wholesome and nutritious food, early rising, and attention to the care of the depurative organs. Snuff, coffee, strong tea, and alcoholic drinks should be prohibited. . . . Hot and crowded rooms, the dissipations of society, and all causes of excitement, including the reading of novels, should be shunned. . . . A change of residence from town to country, a sea voyage, a long journey, a residence abroad, or anything of the sort to bring a new set of influences to bear upon the nervous system is sometimes attended with very fair results.[58]

Trips and voyages, changes of residence, and living abroad were options that were available only to those in comfortable financial situations, and these "treatments" indicate that "hysteria" was a term generally reserved for a condition of wealthy patients.

Since the symptoms of hysteria were often described as more intense versions of the emotions of everyday life, medical and reformist polemics served to exacerbate the tensions of women whose expectations and responsibilities did not correspond to the realities of their environment. Women's lives were a series of paradoxes. They were vested with the power and the responsibility to nurture their children, husband, and nation, yet they were characterized as fragile beings, unable to bear the burden as their noble ancestors had. One influential sector of advisors—reformers and physicians—told them to be healthy for the sake of their children. Another equally powerful group—fashion advisors and etiquette experts—urged them to look pale and delicate, and to dress in a manner which limited movement and symbolized material well-being. It is not altogether surprising that both women and their physicians sought refuge in the vaguely medical and covertly political maladies of neurasthenia and hysteria.

89. Jayne's Carminative contained more alcohol than "Lydia Pinkham's," and also a small amount of another popular compound for the cure of ills, opium. Patent medicine, Dr. D. Jayne and Son, Philadelphia, c. 1885.

SIX

CYCLING and the SOCIAL GRACES

THE
NEW LEISURE

Day after day, for over thirty years, Almira MacDonald recorded her social calls in her diary. Some days she made as many as sixteen separate visits to friends and relations, often staying no longer than the time required to leave a calling card.[1] She was typical of women of her middle-class milieu, venturing forth each afternoon to keep her circle of social contacts alive, even if only by means of a formal gesture. Calling—paying ritualized visits to friends—was the most important leisure activity for middle-class women in the post–Centennial era. It was a complex and mannered procedure by which people identified their social intentions and maintained or sought to overcome class distinctions.

MacDonald might leave her calling card and two of her husband's as a gesture of courtesy or she might stay for the full thirty minutes of a proper visit. In either case, she was indicating that she wished to maintain social relations. To be proper and considerate, she made her calls between three and five o'clock in the afternoon. Visits early in the morning, late in the evening, at meal times, or when someone would ordinarily be engaged in household or business duties, were improper.[2]

As the well-educated wife of a moderately prosperous lawyer and the mother of two daughters and a son, MacDonald knew the ritualized vocabulary of calling cards. By folding the upper right corner, she signified that she had come in person rather than sending the card by way of a second party. Folding the upper left corner of the card meant congratulations; folding the lower right corner, goodbye; and the lower left corner, condolence. If she folded the entire left end of the card, she was indicating that she had intended to visit all the women in the family, rather than only her peer.

There was also an elaborate calling-card etiquette for the receiver of visits. If MacDonald did not wish to receive a certain visitor, she would instruct a servant or other surrogate to announce that she was not at home or that she was "engaged." When the visitor left a card, she ignored it. By not returning the visitor's card with one of her own or with a visit, she could express her distaste without the unpleasantness of a confrontation. These indirect methods of communication also allowed MacDonald to attempt some social climbing without too much danger of embarrassment. She took a small gamble by politely calling on a family of acknowledged higher social standing and leaving her card and that of her husband. If she was favored by her "betters," her card was returned with a visit, and she had "made it."

This mannered domestic drama took place in the front hall, which had to be clean and impressive, especially if MacDonald was trying to impress her social superiors. On a hall table or on part of the hall stand, MacDonald placed a card-receiver. Essentially a tray or dish on a stand, card-receivers became popular in the 1870s and were available in many styles, materials (silver was especially popular),

90. Callers wishing to pay respects or perhaps to begin an acquaintance left their calling cards on a card receiver in the front hall. Silver plate. Parker, Casper and Company, Meriden, Connecticut, c. 1867–1869.

and sizes, from a few inches to over a foot in diameter (Fig. 90). True to the canons of propriety, MacDonald would never have displayed the cards of socially prominent people around the edge of the hall mirror in order to impress visitors with her status.[3]

There were other "errands" which got women out of the house and into a more public sphere. Shopping in one of the urban innovations of post–Civil War America—the department store—reinforced the role of women as the chief consumers of middle-class culture. These large stores with everything gathered together under one roof replaced many of the small specialty shops of the city, and dramatically changed the shopping habits of middle-class American women (Fig. 91). By purchasing an extensive assortment of goods in bulk and by maintaining a cash-only policy, these businesses could offer slightly lower prices as lures for customers. They also offered such services as package delivery, jewelry and watch repair, and even fur storage, a special boon for apartment and other city dwellers with limited storage space.

Large urban department stores were monumental edifices with plush and ornate trimmings. There were luxurious waiting rooms for ladies, art galleries, even ladies' writing rooms with current newspapers. Some stores had

91. This souvenir bookmark shows one of Rochester, New York's largest department stores. At the turn of the century, in cities throughout the United States, these huge emporia offered shoppers a wider variety of goods and services than any previous form of merchandising had provided. Advertising ribbon, woven silk. Rochester, New York, 1909.

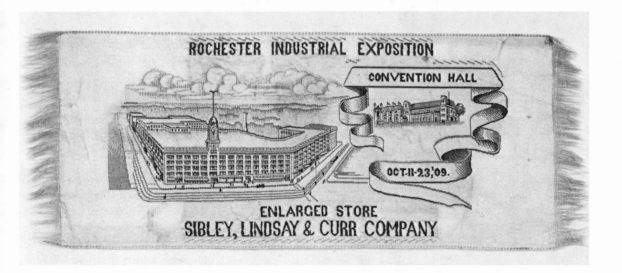

restaurants where women could partake of the extremely popular "ladies' luncheon." Here they visited with friends in an environment that had the protection of home without the burden of display of social graces. It was the best of both worlds.

Shopping was an unstructured form of leisure, which took little advance planning and was socially acceptable. Department stores were the middle-class woman's counterpart to the private men's clubs of the late-nineteenth-century city. Their exclusivity was based on the consumer's ability to afford the goods displayed in the store or offered in the restaurant.

A woman's leisure hours might also be devoted to artistic activities in the home, but there was a strict social code of behavior for these endeavors. Any "artistic creativity other than dabbling" was generally discouraged.[4] Men were the traditional creators of fine arts; women were supposed to be the producers of handicrafts. Watercolor painting and drawing were considered amateur pursuits rather than fine arts, and were proper ladylike activities. Young women were expected to fill the blank pages of albums they were given with their own and their friends' paintings, usually landscapes and realistic renditions of flowers. Technical virtuosity—copying—rather than originality was the admired quality of this work. Painting and drawing were taught in schools, and articles published in popular ladies' magazines went beyond the "how-to" stage and spoke of the importance of painting as a means of fostering a love of beauty in children.[5]

Women often did handiwork or mending with friends or family, and sometimes took their sewing boxes when visiting, thereby relieving the monotony of the work with conversation. In the proliferation of instruction books and magazine articles published in the last half of the nineteenth century, women could find detailed instructions for making such practical objects as baskets, match safes, fire screens, and wall pockets (Figs. 99 and 93). Wall pockets served as hiding places for dust rags, magazines, newspapers, or any other item a woman wanted to keep readily accessible but out of sight until needed. They were fashioned of wood, cardboard, or straw, then painted and gilded, or covered with fabric or leather.

In wall-hung shadowboxes and in glass-domed decorative pieces which were placed on tables and mantels, women displayed their manual dexterity, cultivated taste, and socioeconomic status (they had the leisure time to devote to artistic pursuits because of domestic help). Both the shadowboxes and the pieces under glass (called "shades") functioned a little "exhibits" of women's ability to imitate nature (cloth birds and feather or wax flowers) or to create something purely decorative (shellwork pictures and jewelry) (Fig. 94).

Parks, the shore, specialty shops, or even the streets were sources for the seeds, moss, twigs, grasses, shells, and other materials for these creations. One popular decorative form employed leaf skeletons: dried leaves were soaked in water until pulpy, then scrubbed with a brush until only their skeletons remained. Women then dried the leaf skeletons, arranged them artistically, and placed the creation under glass domes to grace the parlor or dining room (Fig. 95).

Reading fiction and poetry were popular leisure activities for women. Religious novels, like Lew Wallace's *Ben Hur* (1880) or Elizabeth Stuart Phelps' *The Gates Ajar* (1868) were sanctioned by moral critics because of the pious content of the works. "Romantic" novels, though condemned by physicians and reformers, were extremely popular.[6] Women eagerly bought and read such sentimental tales as Rhoda Broughton's *Belinda* (1883), in which a tough, passionate heroine is jilted by a lover who claims he is too poor to marry. Distraught and somewhat cynical, she marries a pedantic Oxford graduate. The match proves so distasteful that the couple stays together for only three days. Later, the original suitor returns (now a wealthy man), and the lovers resume their affair. The illicit and "illegal" love triumphs when the Oxford man dies.[7]

Like the heroine of *Belinda,* the protagonists of Mrs. E. D. E. N. Southworth, the largest-selling woman novelist

92. The center panel of this fire screen was embroidered by hand, perhaps according to a preprinted pattern. The woodwork was factory-made. Fire screens were used to deflect intense heat from a fireplace. Walnut, with embroidered panel of cotton, velvet, and wool. American, c. 1880.

in nineteenth-century America, were strong, manipulative, and sensual women. Usually they expressed their defiance through an affair of the heart, but occasionally they resorted to more violent means to end their miseries—even murder. The murderess always faced some sort of retribution, but it was seldom discussed at length, and readers were expected to sympathize with the plight of the woman who was driven to the crime. The popularity of these "new" heroines was an expression of latent protest by women against a society in which they had few options and little power to effect their own destiny. Hostility toward men, the church, and marriage—sentiments which were totally unacceptable in conventional society—were condoned in a fictional framework.

In the late nineteenth century more and more middle-class women also began to attend classes, either in a formal educational setting or in the homes of individuals who taught their specialties. During the winter of 1895, Lollie Osborne of Canandaigua, New York, was "at Literature class," "at reading class at Lizzie Simonds," and "at Astronomy."[8] Her mother, who was widowed by this time, also attended the astronomy class periodically. Formal or informal classes were a source of mental stimulation and

93. Commercial punched-paper designs for needlework were widely available in the late nineteenth century—displays of a woman's dexterity, though not her creativity. Lithograph motto, American, c. 1870

94. "Shades" and other arrangements of leaves, feathers, or shells were "exhibits" of women's ability to imitate nature. Left: wreath made of dyed goose feathers. Right: shell bouquet. Both were made in American homes, 1850–1885.

a reason to get together for women who otherwise might have been limited to activities in their homes.

Women were to direct the fruits of their reading and study into the service of their families and others who were needy. "And what blessed results would follow to our beloved country," wrote Catherine Beecher, "if all well educated women carried out the principles of Christianity in the exercise of their developed powers."[9] Although it would be incorrect to conclude that the most enjoyable elements of a woman's leisure activities in the late nineteenth century were peripheral to their "real" significance as an extension of duty, it would be an equal distortion to argue that pleasure and relaxation were the only goals and results of recreation. Calling, reading, shopping, studying, and crafts or artwork allowed women the opportunity to exercise a degree of choice, skill, and creativity that housework did not. To some extent these activities—particularly reading and shopping—allowed a woman to enter a larger sphere than that of her home.

As the century drew to a close, the benefits of physical exercise for women as well as men began to be recognized.

95. Skeleton leaves, virtually unknown to Americans of today, were considered one of the greatest indicators of a woman's manual dexterity and artistic talents in the late nineteenth century. American, c. 1875.

Although strenuous and competitive sports were generally discouraged, and clothing fashions sometimes prevented participation, a variety of sports and games were open to women for the first time. Maintaining the health of white Anglo-Saxon Protestant women for the preservation of their families and "race" was important, but the simple enjoyment of play and movement was also sanctioned by the arbiters of modern family life.

Walking was the simplest form of exercise, and because it required no special equipment, clothing, or travel, it was open to women of all classes. Clothing guidelines for walking and hiking were simple: loose upper garments and a skirt short enough to avoid dragging were sufficient, although walking skirts with a system of hooks and eyes to hold up the front could be purchased for traversing rough or steep terrain.[10]

Another inexpensive and accessible form of exercise was the use of Indian clubs. "As a means of exercise, both pleasing and beneficial," wrote S. D. Kehoe, author of *The Indian Club Exercises* (1866), "there is nothing for ladies

96. A class photograph of young women with their exercise materials—wands, rings, and dumbbells. American, c. 1880.

97. Croquet's contained movements made it an ideal sport for women, whose clothing made any exertion almost impossible. Painted plaster figurine. M. J. Morris Company, American, c. 1877.

more suitable and simple than the Indian Clubs." Invalids and children used the short and light club, also called a "bat," and adults used the long club, or Indian club proper. Clubs were used in pairs and usually were from twenty-four to twenty-eight inches long, and weighed between four and twenty pounds each. They were used as barbells and weight-training machines are used now—to build up muscle tone and strength. Ladies used lighter-weight clubs than men, and did the same exercises, starting with simple lifts and working up to more difficult ones. Proper dress was loose so that one's arms were free to move in any position and one's chest could expand. Indian club exercises were probably more work than sport, since the goal of the exercise was to "promote the natural development of a graceful form and movement" (Fig. 96).[11]

Croquet was introduced in England in 1856 and was probably brought to America in the early 1860s (Fig. 97). It was considered particularly suitable for women since it required considerable skill but not too much strength or technique. (Women were allegedly deficient in both.) Although croquet was never a popular men's game, it had both social and economic advantages: men and women could play together, and it required little equipment and no special clothing.

Roller skating was introduced in 1863, and it was quickly made fashionable by the elite of New York City (Fig. 98).[12] By the 1870s rinks with hard maple floors had

98. Roller skating rinks became extremely popular at the turn of the century. Women's fashions were adapted to accommodate the sport, and courting couples could take advantage of the physical contact that skating together allowed. Metal and wood roller skates. Barney and Berry Company, Springfield, Massachusetts, 1876–1883.

been built in nearly every town and city. By paying an admission fee of twenty-five or fifty cents, men, women, and children could participate in races, fancy skating, or dancing on skates. Special skating dresses which allowed more freedom of movement became popular by the 1870s. Indicative of the extent of the craze was this wry comment by the editors of *Harper's Weekly,* in the form of a potential gravestone inscription for a departed skater:

> *Our Jane has climbed the golden stair*
> *And passed the jasper gates;*
> *Henceforth she will have wings to wear,*
> *Instead of roller skates.*[13]

The popularity of roller skating waned by the 1890s, but, like ice skating, it helped lead to more freedom in dress and behavior for women (Fig. 99).

99. Like roller skating, ice skating allowed couples the privacy they wanted, as well as an acceptable way to be close to each other. Leather and steel ice skates. Vulcan Skate Company, Philadelphia, c. 1900.

Lawn tennis was another popular sport for middle-class women. At first proper tennis form entailed patting the ball back and forth, without keeping score, but, according to both critics and proponents, players soon were caught up in the competitive spirit of the game, finding it an excellent method of exercise and a useful mental and physical outlet. More active than croquet or archery (which enjoyed a brief popularity in the 1870s), tennis also appealed to men. By the 1880s it had become the rage in fashionable summer resorts, and magazines devoted space to the proper attire to wear while playing. "Tuxedo" suits, knitted of fine wool yarn with trim in a contrasting color, were recommended for tennis by *Godey's* because they were both comfortable and durable.[14]

Rowing and canoeing were popular pastimes, and, like tennis, golf, and riding, necessitated changes in women's costume (Fig. 100). Rowers left their corsets at home. Stout boots, a skirt that barely touched the ground, a flannel shirt, and a sailor hat were recommended. Women were also urged to wear heavy gloves to protect their hands when they rowed. Competitive rowing was popular among men, but for women rowing was supposed to be strictly for exercise and pleasure.

Many women went to beaches, but few of them actually swam. Ready-made bathing suits were constructed in two pieces—drawers and a tunic—and usually were made of nonclinging fabrics like flannel, jersey, soft serge, or even heavy mohair (Fig. 101). To complete the bathing costume, women wore full-length stockings, bathing shoes, and even a ruffled cap. Weighted down with heavy, voluminous fabrics, all but the strongest swimmer would have been

100. This painting depicts a woman paddling her own canoe in a perhaps unusually self-assured manner. Silkscreen image on canvas, artist unknown. American, c. 1905.

101. Bathing costumes differed only slightly in appearance from everyday wear, but were much less bulky, though the volume of clothing was enormous compared with bathing wear today. Bathing costumes from *Godey's Lady's Book,* July 1875.

exhausted after a few strokes. Until the twentieth century, most women did not experience real swimming.

Some sports, such as horseback riding and golf, were available only to the wealthy, or to those willing to make financial sacrifices for social aspirations. Riding necessitated renting or owning and maintaining a horse as well as an elaborate costume; a riding habit, hat, gloves, boots, and equestrienne tights were social necessities for a lady (Fig. 102). Women interested in the sport also had to overcome physicians' warnings that riding might complicate or stimulate pelvic troubles.[15] But for the wealthy and the aspiring middle class (perhaps hoping to have their daughters marry "up"), horseback riding provided both exercise and an expression of social status.

Golf also had enormous appeal to status-conscious women of the middle and wealthy classes, in part because the exclusive golf and country clubs provided such clear affirmations of social success. Golf had all the advantages and none of the drawbacks of riding: it provided an op-

102. Formal riding gloves were a vital part of the total equestrienne gear for a woman rider. Like habits, boots, and hats, they were expensive. Ladies' leather riding gloves. American, c. 1870.

103. Golf was an activity open only to a small number of the middle class. Golfing clubs were almost exclusively private, and were most assuredly discriminating. Most clubs did not allow women to become members themselves. Women could play only as "guests" of their husbands or fathers, and only at certain times during the week. Cast-bronze bookend. American, c. 1910.

portunity to get outside the home and was an excellent means of exercise without so much potential for injury.

There was only one golf course in America in 1890, but by 1900 the game's popularity had so increased that there were more than one thousand courses. Golf began as a man's game, however, and women were allowed to play only during the hours when most men worked. Such was the demand by women that the number of hours was gradually increased, until Saturday afternoon became the only time reserved for men only.

Golf also demanded modified clothing. According to Genevieve Hecker, the American women's golf champion in 1901 and 1902, "common-sense" corsets were acceptable because they were not tightly laced and gave support without hindering free movement or restricting respiration. A cotton shirtwaist blouse and a short (ankle-length) skirt was the most popular outfit for women golfers (Fig. 103). High- or low-cut shoes with low heels and broad, hobnail-studded soles made of leather or rubber were the precursors to modern golf shoes. Women golfers were exempted from the usual hat requirement, and most women golfers played without gloves.[16]

Outdoor camping—essentially a rustic version of middle-class home life—became a popular vacation activity for many Victorian men and women, especially after the publication of W. H. H. Murray's *Adventures in the Wilderness* in 1869. This extremely popular book stimulated what contemporaries called "Murray's Rush" to such areas as the Catskills, the Adirondacks, and the White Mountains. For a party of six or eight people (considered the ideal number), there would be several tents, one designated as a dining and drawing room, the others for sleeping. Some campers brought cots or made beds by filling empty mattress and pillow tickings with boughs or other available materials. Campers were urged to take blue, red, or gray blankets (which did not show dust), and a two- or three-yard strip of old carpet to cover the ground in the center of the tent. Camp chairs, steamer chairs, and hammocks provided comfortable seating, and smart campers transported their equipment in boxes and flat trunks that could double as washstands, cupboards, tables, and extra seating.[17]

Properly equipped visitors to the woods packed plated eating utensils and earthenware rather than tin dishes. Some campers expected to secure food through hunting and fishing, but, wrote *Godey's* in 1888, "if contiguous to civilization, the country butcher will be glad to bring to your door all the fresh meat, poultry, vegetables, and fruit you may wish, two or three times a week; . . . butter, milk, and eggs can be procured at some neighboring farmhouse." Cooking was done either on an oil stove, on a sheet-iron "army-oven," or over a campfire. To attend to personal cleanliness, inexpensive washbasins and pitchers, usually made of a pressed paper material known as "fibre-ware," were available. Not only were they lighter than ceramic sets, they were much less fragile and far more practical to use in the "wilds."[18]

Camping clothes for women were carefully delineated in fashion magazines (Fig. 104). "The camp is a capital place to wear out one's old clothing, provided that it is stylish looking," claimed *Godey's*. Wool or flannel dresses in any color but black were recommended for cold-weather camping, and seersucker suits or dresses were the critics' choice for summer excursions. For lounging, "A loose gingham or flannel wrapper will be found a great convenience to rest in during the heat of the day," while a rubber outfit was a necessity in wet weather. Linen or celluloid collars and cuffs or colored silk handkerchiefs tucked inside at the neck helped protect dresses from becoming soiled in an environment where there were no washing facilities. The fashionable ladies' camping outfit was completed with a tam-o'-shanter or peaked red, white, or blue felt hat; dark stockings; and low-heeled boots or shoes with thick soles. Gloves were not considered necessary. Civilization, however, was never to be too distant: fashion magazines suggested that lady campers take a stylish traveling dress with them for any journeys into town (Fig. 105).[19]

104. Camping clothes were less complex than everyday city wear, in deference to the necessities of "roughing it." But practicality went only so far: corsets, long skirts, and bustles were still the order of the day. Ladies' "mountain suit" from *Godey's Lady's Book,* July 1883.

105. Traveling clothes, like camping garments, were stripped-down versions of "at home" wear. Ruffles and voluminous petticoats were eliminated. Ladies' traveling dress from *Peterson's Magazine,* May 1892.

Women's activities while camping were essentially a re-creation of their city or town lives. They were in charge of all housekeeping, and still mistresses of the "kitchen," though male companions probably cleaned whatever game and fish were caught. Moreover, a vacation from the city or suburban household did not mean women were free to reject the ethic of continuous worthwhile activities. In an article propounding the healthful benefits of camping, the editors of *Godey's* maintained that "with a constant round of systematized work and play, there will be no idle hours" (Figs. 106 and 107).[20]

The advent of the bicycle in the 1880s stimulated great controversy about women's proper role in society. Questions of "how they should ride, when they should ride, who they should ride with" were considered by commentators, and "wheeling's" many critics were certain that bicycle riding threatened women's health, morals, and rep-

106. Handling firearms was an acceptable activity on holiday, but the corset and bustle were not dispensed with. "Two Women Hunting Wild Fowl," oil on canvas, artist unknown. American, c. 1885.

utation. Critics opposed wearing union suits (to absorb perspiration) or bloomers, and worried about the privacy and potential liberty bicycling granted to young men and women. Physicians Thomas Lothrop and William Potter posited that the bicycle inevitably promoted immodesty in women, and could potentially harm their reproductive systems. Other critics argued that women bicyclists favored shorter skirts, thus "inviting" insults and advances. Moreover, by tilting the bicycle seat, they could "beget or foster the habit of masturbation." For advocates like Maria E. Ward, however, "The bicycle [was] an educational factor . . . creating the desire for progress, the preference for what is better, the striving for the best, broadening the intelligence and intensifying love of home and country."[21]

Before such noble attributes could be encouraged by "the wheel," change in dress or the design of bicycles was necessary. Skirts made riding the Ordinary (a bicycle with

107. Fishing was also considered a sport for women. The ideal situation included a guide to power and navigate the boat, as well as to bait the hook and remove the fish. Oil on board, artist unknown. American, c. 1885.

a large front wheel) virtually impossible (Fig. 108). Tricycles, however, were designed to accommodate full skirts and allowed women to ride without adopting the bloomer outfit (Fig. 109), which many women opposed for its politically radical associations. Like nearly every other aspect of life in the nineteenth century, tricycle riding had a specific set of rules and regulations. The rule against women riding alone in fact generated a new profession: the professional lady cyclist as chaperone. Tricycles were commonly used for touring, and the tandem tricycle was popular with couples (Fig. 110).

The first bicycle with two equal-size wheels and a dropped frame with no crossbar was the Victor, first manufactured in 1887 (Fig. 111). With the addition of pneumatic tires (invented in 1889) and enclosed gears, women were able to ride comfortably without their skirts becoming entangled. The final dramatic improvement in bicycle technology was the coaster brake, invented in 1898. These features enabled women to bicycle safely without having to don bloomers.

By 1900 bicycle manufacturers, sales agencies, and private individuals had opened women's velocipede or riding schools in many northeastern cities. The Metropolitan Academy in New York City set aside a special area of its hall for women wishing to learn the mysteries of wheeling,

108. The "Ordinary Bicycle" required extraordinary balance, and women's clothing of the era made it almost impossible for them to ride. Rubber, steel, and leather bicycle. Pope Manufacturing Company, Hartford, Connecticut, c. 1888.

109. The tricycle was easier for a woman to ride without going counter to popular dress codes. (Advocates of the "radical" bloomers were widely criticized.) Wood, steel, and rubber tricycle. American, c. 1895.

110. A lithograph celebrating one of America's most popular new sports. Untitled, by H. Sandham. L. Prang and Company, Boston, c. 1887.

111. With equal-sized wheels, a dropped middle bar, pneumatic tires, fenders, and brakes, the safety bicycle enabled women to ride comfortably without entangling their skirts. Safety bicycle, steel, tin, rubber, and leather. Hendee Manufacturing Company, Springfield, Massachusetts, c. 1910.

and installed the first athletics-linked shower baths for women in America. The Michaux Club, a New York City organization founded in 1895, provided women with riding lessons in the morning, music to accompany indoor riding after lunch, and afternoon tea in the clubroom. The club also provided "ten pin rides" in which women demonstrated their skill by riding slalom-fashion through lines of bowling pins set on the foor.[22] Indoor riding for women was more acceptable to critics than outdoor bicycling because it was controlled; there was neither the possibility of young couples riding off in private, nor any chance of immodest exposure of woman's limbs. Men were excluded from the women's bicycling sessions.

In 1895 a good bicycle cost approximately one hundred dollars. In some families the bicycle replaced the piano as a necessary accoutrement to middle-class life. For those who could not afford to buy a bicycle, rental establishments flourished, and many women rented bicycles for an afternoon ride in the park. In 1896, at the height of the craze, one enterprising manufacturer even brought out a bicycle for those in mourning. With a black ebony finish and no nickel or steel for decoration, it was advertised as being proper for widows.[23]

An elaborate system of guidelines was established for the woman cyclist who ventured outside her neighborhood. She was not to speak to strangers, although she could accept help should her bicycle break down. The proper lady took a broken bicycle to the nearest repair shop rather than waiting along the road for a helpful gentleman to pass by. As with tricycling, solitary riding was forbidden, and a lady shared a tandem bicycle only with a man, never with another woman. When a man and a woman rode together on separate bicycles, the woman was always to ride in front, permitting the man to be aware of any difficulties she might be having. Only when attempting to ride up a hill was it proper for the gentleman to ride ahead. By preceding his companion, he could use a tow rope to assist her up the hill should she find the going difficult or impossible. Men were also charged with

protecting women from marauding dogs; in the 1890s the
ammonia gun was advertised as the perfect weapon for
this task.[24]

Arbiters of fashion prescribed a specific costume for
cycling, for, as Mrs. M. Cooke wrote in 1896, "It is impossible to do good work or to practice comfortably unless
you are properly dressed." For women tricyclists, *Godey's*
recommended a straight, side-pleated skirt of serge, worn
over one underskirt and full trousers lined with flannel
and made of material to match the dress. A warm jersey
and jacket trimmed with fur, with a "tricyclist's" cap to
match, completed the outfit. For riding in tandem, the
stylish woman might wear a suit corresponding in color
to that of her gentleman companion. Gray, brown, dark
green, or navy wool were the most popular colors, and
were worn with white flannel shirts and white helmets. In
Bicycling for Ladies (1896), Maria Ward recommended a
lightly boned but uncorseted blouse, a serge skirt, low
shoes with spats (to keep the gravel out), and a walking
hat with a few unobtrusive quills. Cooke favored a cycling
costume known as the "londonderry." Made of gray-green
hopsack—a coarse, loosely woven fabric of cotton or
wool—the coat had long, full sides which formed a kind
of skirt when riding. This was worn over full knicker-
bockers and with either a shirt or a double-breasted
"cloth" (wool) or leather vest. In addition, the well-dressed
woman also wore leggings, a hat, doeskin gloves, and a
pair of the broad, low, rubber-soled cycling shoes which
had first come on the market in 1891. A bicycle belt, from
which hung a small leather purse, completed the outfit.
Ward urged any woman taking a bicycling trip or expe-
dition (defined as any trip over an hour in length) to outfit
her bicycle with a lamp, and to pack matches, tools, a
repair kit, sewing materials, and first-aid supplies.[25]

By the late 1880s two- or three-day tours under the
aegis of regional or national cycling groups were common
middle-class activities. In both Europe and America these
organizations charged small membership fees and issued
road books which provided information about routes,

road conditions, hotels, repair shops, and "consuls"—club members in towns and cities, appointed to answer the questions of touring cyclers. Far fewer women than men belonged to these groups, but they evidently participated with equal enthusiasm. In 1888 the Philadelphia Tricyclists Club had 118 members, eighteen of whom were women. That year the club's "Captain's Cup," annually awarded to the member who covered the most miles during the year, was won by a woman "for her mileage record of 3,304 1/4 miles."[26]

The range of leisure activities for women in turn-of-the-century America—from the highly structured system of "calling" to more casual but still mannered sports—broadened as the amount of free time increased. Leisure broke down many of the barriers between the male and female worlds, offering new opportunities for shared experiences for men and women. In addition, sports and bicycling helped women to break free from the confines of the corset, and, beyond that, from the rigid roles into which they had been cast. The time for leisure that the male world of industrialism created for the middle class ultimately helped undo some of the gender-linked underpinnings of that very system.

SEVEN

Visiting ill or dying relatives and friends was an expected and socially required part of the woman's "sphere," part of the broad set of nurturing responsibilities with which she was charged. In 1870 Almira MacDonald listed twenty-six calls on the ill (most in winter); in 1885 she noted twenty-two such calls. She listed herself as ill thirty-four times in 1870, and twenty-nine times in 1885, but her sicknesses did not necessarily prevent her from visiting others.[1] In the late nineteenth century, home, rather than the hospital, was the place for convalescence and death.

Lack of accurate knowledge about the causes and treatment of serious diseases meant that death, especially of children, regularly intruded into everyday life. MacDonald recorded the deaths of seven neighbors or family members in both 1870 and 1885. She attended ten of the fourteen funerals, missing three because they were held in distant cities and one because she herself was ill. In 1867 Alcesta Huntington wrote her mother that a neighbor's child had died of a "fever," and Carolyn T. Lyon, a wealthy woman of the same city, lost two of her babies, one at birth (in 1897), and the other to bronchial pneumonia (in 1901).

In 1868 Alcesta Huntington wrote to her mother that "scarlet fever is very prevalent." Fifteen months later, Alcesta received a letter from her sister, Susan Hooker, telling her that the disease was again rampant. "At Edward's Louie and Bertie have had the scarlet fever and Mary has just lost another little boy and is quite sick. Here we are all well and have great cause for being thankful as there is a great deal of sickness. All the children at cousin Julie's house had the measles."[2]

Census data reinforce the conclusion that the experiences of these women were more typical than exceptional. There were major epidemics of cholera in northeastern cities in 1832, 1849, and 1866, and periodic outbreaks of typhoid, typhus, diphtheria, and such childhood diseases as scarlet fever, measles, and mumps were common. Diphtheria was especially prevalent in 1863 and 1864, between 1874 and 1882, and in 1889; typhoid ravaged the Northeast in the mid-1860s and in 1872. Smallpox claimed fewer lives than either, but was especially virulent in 1872 and 1873, which were also years of exceptionally lethal outbreaks of measles.[3]

In New York City in 1853, forty-nine percent of those who died were children under five. Nearly one-third of Massachusetts women born in the United States in 1850 died before they were twenty; eighty percent of that group (that is, twenty-four percent of the total female population) never reached the age of five (Fig. 112). The mortality rate for children and young women steadily declined throughout the late nineteenth century, but not precipitously; twenty-six percent of all women born in 1890 were dead by 1910.[4] Once they had passed through childhood, men lived longer. The average male infant in Massachusetts in 1878 had a life expectancy of forty-one years and eight months. In the same year, the average twenty-year-old male could expect to live until he was sixty-two years and two months old.[5]

The lives of nineteenth-century women were threatened first by the diseases of childhood, then by an obstacle to survival that was uniquely theirs—childbearing. Women were much more likely than men to die between the ages of twenty-five and fifty-five. The percentage of mothers who died before they reached the age of fifty-five remained high in the nineteenth century and only began to show a marked decrease for women born in 1920. What we now consider a "typical life cycle" for a woman—marrying, having children, and surviving at least until the last child leaves home—was not typical for Massachusetts women born in 1850, 1870, and 1890. Only twenty-three percent of the women born in 1850 lived through the "typical" cycle; and less than twenty-eight percent of the women born in 1890 did. The generation of women born in 1920 is the first in which a majority (fifty-seven percent) lived until their children had grown up.[6]

Since most births occurred at home, and women were expected to visit their neighbors during illnesses and crises, they were likely to witness the death of other women in childbirth. The shared experience of the pain of childbirth

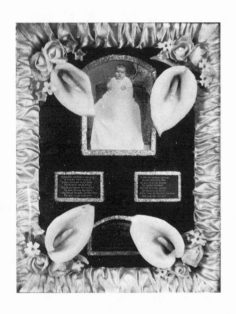

112. This memorial to a deceased infant combines both the technology of mass production and individual handwork. The frame, the photographic image, and the printed sentiments are the work of a machine. The ribbon trimming and the wax flowers are handwork. Memorial decoration for Nellie Popp, deceased 1889, aged 8 months, 14 days.

and the frequency of birth-related death may help explain the declining birthrate in an era when mechanical contraception was virtually unknown and when popular belief held that women did not ovulate in the middle of the menstrual cycle. "Victorian prudery" may have been as much a response to fears of pregnancy and death as a manifestation of middle- and upper-middle-class moral values.

In the 1870s ideas about nature, the family, and heaven had evolved gradually into a more secular, mannered vision than that of the early decades of the nineteenth century. The image of heaven, for example, had become that of the ideal human society, rather than an organic and sacred counterpoint to American society. Heaven was still the kingdom of God, but the image of the realm gradually became more like the perfect suburban home than an ethereal dominion. Before 1800, little had been written or preached about heaven. In Puritan theology, at least, few were destined for that reward; election was at the mercy of God, and was not necessarily a result of human good works. But by the middle of the nineteenth century, such nonevangelical ministers as William Ellery Channing, Andrew Peabody, and Austin Phelps described heaven as a place in which families were reunited, homes restored, and nurseries existed to care for children who died before their parents. The ultimate expression of this view of heaven is in the extremely popular works of Elizabeth Stuart Phelps, whose first important work, *The Gates Ajar* (1868), was set in heaven.

The Gates Ajar describes heaven in minute detail: readers are informed about food, courtship, lifestyles, occupations, and the nature of childcare. The book was a popular success, and Phelps followed it with a series of other works in a similar vein, including *Beyond the Gates* (1883), *Songs of the Silent World* (1885), and *The Struggle for Immortality* (1889).

The conviction that heaven was a perfect extension of life was also manifested in burial procedures of the late nineteenth century. Funerals commonly took place outside the family home in specialized houses of the dead—funeral parlors or funeral homes—under the direction of a new professional, the funeral director. The decay of the corpse, which had earlier been accepted as part of an inevitable cycle of "some ulterior purpose of reproduction" and "eternal circle of creation," was, by 1870, something to be avoided. Arterial embalming and the practice of presenting the body clothed and seemingly asleep, replaced the earlier use of the shroud, which wrapped the untreated corpse. So, too, the wooden coffin was superseded by the metal casket, which was adorned with elaborate hardware, sealed, and guaranteed against leakage (Figs. 113 and 114).

113. The term "casket" as applied to a container for a corpse was relatively new in the late nineteenth century. This firm used both "casket" and "coffin" to avoid confusion. Trade catalog, Stolts, Russell and Company, New York, c. 1880.

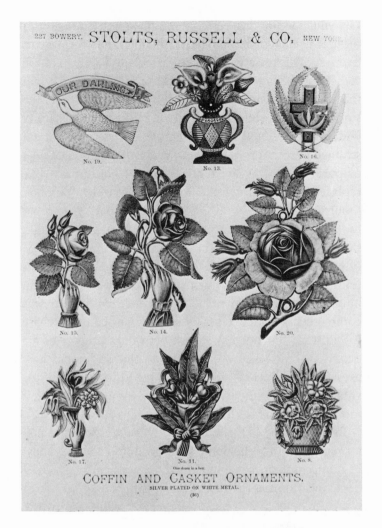

114. The lily and the cut rose, widely recognized symbols of death in the nineteenth century, were used as decorations on coffins and caskets. Trade catalog, Stolts, Russell and Company, New York, c. 1880.

These elaborate preparations were not immune from criticism. One critic bluntly pointed out the inconsistency in American health habits and funeral practices.

It seems to me we prize the body far more after its use for us is at an end than while it is ours to use. We do not neglect the dead, we dress them in beautiful garments, we adorn them with flowers, we follow them to the grave with religious ceremonies, we build costly monuments to place over their graves, and then we go to weep over their last resting place.[7]

Grieving for the dead in clothing designed especially for mourning linked the family together and set them apart from secular society, much as fenced-in family plots in cemeteries isolated them from other families. Black was the socially appropriate color for mourning, as it had been since at least the sixteenth century. Late-nineteenth-century widows were expected to wear black garments of restrained decoration in their first year of mourning. Shades of purple and gray or combinations of black and white replaced black during the following year of "second" mourning. Jewelry was an acceptable part of proper mourning dress if it conformed to the canons of restraint. Black glass or semi-precious stones and mementos made of woven human hair were the most popular jewelry forms (Fig. 115). By the 1870s women could find instruction in hair weaving in *Godey's,* and ready-made hair jewelry was commercially available for those who wished to purchase it (Fig. 116). Intended as a more personal memento of the deceased, hair jewelry—rather than the traditional lock preserved in a locket—represented the introduction of the values of adornment and handicraft skills into one of life's most significant rites of passage.

By the middle of the nineteenth century, decorative memorial devices for the home were produced commercially. Printing companies manufactured memorial prints, usually depicting mourners at a gravestone, with blank lines which

115. Jewelry made of woven human hair, or containing a lock of hair, was popular among American women during the late nineteenth century. Some of this jewelry was meant to memorialize loved ones who had died. Top: mourning bracelet, gold and woven hair. American, c. 1860. Left: mourning brooch, gold, hair, and glass. American, c. 1870. Right: mourning brooch, gold, glass, leather, and woven hair. American, c. 1870. Bottom: mourning bracelet, gold, glass, and woven hair, tintype miniature. American c. 1865–1875.

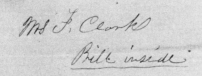

FOR THE LADIES.

We all preserve the Hair of deceased or absent friends, as a precious memento, but to **MRS. C. S. WILBUR** belongs the merit of turning the plain Souvenir into sets of **ORNAMENTS**, of the most becoming and beautiful character. The perfection to which this new Art has been brought, has led to the general adoption of these Ornaments by the LADIES. To say nothing of the pleasant idea of thus

WEARING THE HAIR OF THOSE WE LOVE AND CHERISH,

is incomparably superior to Metalic Jewelry, no person of good taste will venture to deny. MOTHERS who thus wear Bracelets of their Children's Hair, most ingeniously wrought, and in many instances of

ELABORATE

NECKLACES,

Broaches, Rings, GENTLEMEN's Guard and Fob Chains, Charms and Ear Rings, &c., &c., of the same. CHILDREN, to wear the Hair of

DEPARTED PARENTS,

or of those still with them,—to our mind there is nothing more agreeable as a token or keepsake than can be produced in this manner, by the skillful hands of those who have acquired this curious art of manufacture, and who now practice it in such perfection in this country, &c.

116. Advertisement for memorial hair jewelry. American, c. 1880.

117. Memorial prints were mass-produced and inexpensive. A popular form of commemoration, they were often hung on parlor walls. The common Christian symbols of mourning—the weeping willow, the cross and the church, roses, and morning glories— were depicted on most prints. Lithographed memorial print. J. Baillie, New York, c. 1849.

could be filled in with the name and life dates of the deceased (Fig. 117). These prints replaced the earlier stylized paintings which had first come into fashion after the death of George Washington in 1799. Hung on the parlor wall, they were constant reminders of the deceased, notices to visitors of a family's continuing grief.

In the month after a funeral, widows were expected to remain at home, except to attend church. During the remainder of the first year they could leave their homes

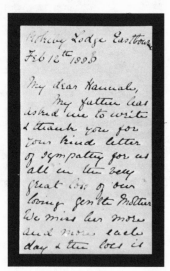

118. Mourning stationery with a wide black border indicated that the bereaved was in the first year of mourning. The width of the black line was decreased the second year. English and American mourning stationery c. 1870–1900.

without social censure, but attendance at celebrations or other explicitly pleasurable occasions was considered in poor taste. During the first year of mourning, friends, family, and others could express their sympathy by visiting with the bereaved or by leaving calling cards. Proper response to such callers was made on cards bordered in black (Fig. 118). The most fashion-conscious women began their year of mourning using cards having one-quarter-inch borders, and decreased the thickness of the black line as they neared the end of their second year of mourning, when they began full reentry into society. The periods of acceptable mourning for relatives other than spouses were shorter: mourning for parents and children lasted one year; six months was appropriate for grandparents and siblings.

As death began to be thought of as a customs inspection on the way to the eternal vacation in the comfortable suburban cottage, deep mourning received critical scrutiny. In 1859 Henry Ward Beecher, perhaps the most influential clergyman of his day, urged: "Draw not over yourselves the black tokens of pollution. Do not blaspheme by naming that despair which is triumph and eternal life." Beecher was one of the earliest advocates of the celebration of death as a gift, since he had come to reject the existence of hell. For him, "Death [was] only God's call, 'Come home.' "[8] Similarly, in "Imprisoned," a popular poem of 1873:

> When the angel of death, like the loving child,
> Proposes to set us free;
> We shrink back in anguish and terror wild,
> And would still a prisoner be.[9]

But Beecher's advice to abandon black, and his own funeral of lilies and white and red roses, did not eradicate black as the common mourning color. In a section of the March 1873 issue of *Godey's* entitled "Chitchat," the author asserts that "black, spite of all that has been said to the contrary, remains the first choice with most persons."[10] The use of flowers at funeral services appears to have increased in the late nineteenth century, but the continuation of formal mourning practices indicates that few accepted death joyfully.

Mourning etiquette for men was less rigorously defined, and their actions less circumscribed, in part because of the demands of the middle-class commercial world. Mourning and grieving were by definition expressions of sentiment and emotion, aspects of human behavior which the nineteenth century relegated to the preserve of women. Moreover, death was a religious issue, and by the 1870s, religion itself had become the domain and responsibility of women.

During the first of the widespread evangelical revivals in America (the Great Awakening of the 1740s), women and men participated with equal fervor. By the middle of the nineteenth century, however, the majority of active church members were women. Church membership had grown dramatically in the preceding century, from a tiny percentage of the population in 1750, to one-fifteenth in 1800, and nearly one-fourth in 1860. By 1910, over forty percent of the American public were church members. Most of the new churchgoers joined the evangelical sects— the Methodists and the Baptists—or the Roman Catholic Church, and most of them were women. This pattern of involvement was probably the result of the evangelical methods of nineteenth-century revivalist ministers, who emphasized the role of women as the pious, nurturing members of the race.[11]

> That they [women] are more religious than men is proven by their preponderance in all the churches; that they are more pitiful [*sic*], more gentle, more attached to family, and better fitted to train children, who will deny?[12]

The link between women's roles and religion was elaborately defined by one of the most popular advisors of the era, Josiah Gilbert Holland.

> God meant that you should be dependent upon men, and that in this dependence should exist some of your

119. Images of motherhood, religion, and death were often mingled in the nineteenth century. The vase of cut roses below the painting of the child on the wall suggests that the painting may be a memorial portrait. "Maternal Piety," lithograph. Nathaniel Currier, New York, c. 1860.

profoundest and sweetest attractions and your noblest characteristics. Your bodies are smaller than those of men. You were not made to wrestle with the rough forces of nature. You were not made for war, nor commerce, nor agriculture. . . . Man has his sphere—woman hers. . . . Now if you will go with me into a circle of praying Christians, or if you will take up with me a list of the members of any church . . . you will find . . . that at least two-thirds of the members of the prayer meeting are women, and that the church register will show a corresponding proportion of female names. Why is this? Is it because women are weaker than men, simply? . . . It is because a feeling of dependence is native in the female heart. . . . It is because the female mind has to undergo comparatively a small revolution to become religious.[13]

The world of commerce (independence) was thus considered antipathetic to the world of religion.

In the context of this ideological and economic construct, the family and home were a special sort of religious sphere, wherein home was the church, woman was the priestess, and the family (especially the children) were the congregation. "Piety," concluded Holland, "is an absolute necessity to you. You can no more perform those offices to which you are called, properly and efficiently, without piety, than a bird can fly without wings." Piety and motherhood gradually evolved into a nearly interchangeable relationship, often depicted in engravings in the popular magazines of the period (Fig. 119). In such prints as "Maternal Piety," the nurturing role of motherhood and the propensity toward religious feelings were presented as identical. Leaders of the church (generally male) were called "ministers." Women, leaders of the pious home, were to "minister to the poor and the distressed," as well as to their own familial flock.[14]

Religious iconography became increasingly prominent in domestic decoration when religion entered the female domain. In the Northeast, the Gothic revival had begun in the 1840s, and Gothic-style hall chairs, library furniture, paintings, and decorative pieces, such as punched-paper mottos and feather crosses, remained popular throughout the century (Figs. 120, 121, and 122). These pieces were intended to confer a sacred aspect on the home and family.

The celebration of feminine emotion, piety, and sentiment allowed the Protestant clergy and the middle-class woman to become allies in the promulgation of what were defined as the essentially feminine virtues of nurture, generosity, passivity, and moral stewardship. Recognizing the popular passion for imaginative literature, the clerical-feminine alliance attempted to spread the word and control

120. This feather cross was a testament not only to a woman's skill but also to her piety. The representation of morning glories and roses indicates that this is a mourning piece. Feathers and velvet. American, c. 1880.

121. The "Rock of Ages" motif was common in both the commercially produced and the home-crafted arts of the era. Women more frequently than men were depicted clinging to the cross. Reverse painting on glass. American, c. 1870–1900.

the potentially dangerous emotions reading triggered by providing masses of "good" novels. Thus the Reverend E. P. Roe, in his introduction to *From Jest to Earnest* (1875), argued:

> If millions in the impressible period of youth, in spite of all that any can do, will read fiction, then it would be a sacred duty in those who love their kind, to make this food of the forming character healthful and bracing, and ennobling in nature. Earnest men and women, who hold and would transmit the truth, must speak in a way that will secure a hearing.[15]

The basic plot structure of the popular religious novel turned around an individual (or group) whose life was transformed by religion. One genre of the Christian tale was set in the time of Christ; characters (usually unbelievers) came to Judea and actually experienced Christ or a miracle. *Ben Hur,* Lew Wallace's epic of 1880, was the most popular example of this plot pattern, and in fact the largest-selling religious novel of the nineteenth century. The other major type of religious novel was set in contemporary times, and usually detailed the piety and sometimes the martyrdom of men or women surrounded by corruption.

122. Punched-paper mottos, usually emblazoned with religious sentiments, were found in nearly every middle-class home. "God Bless Our Home" wall motto, punched paper and wool thread. American, c. 1860–1880.

Roe was one of several ministers who were successful as novelists. In his best-selling novel *Barriers Burned Away* (1873), a devout young man comes to Chicago and successfully pursues a business career. He falls in love with a woman of society who mocks his piety until he rescues her during the Great Fire of 1871, after which she assumes his manner of devotion. Roe's sequel, *Opening a Chestnut Burr* (1874), had basically the same plot, with the gender roles reversed. It, too, sold well. Roe's novels annually brought him royalties of fifteen thousand dollars in an era when most authors earned approximately two hundred dollars annually per book.[16]

Other ministers who capitalized on the popularity of this form of literature were the Reverends Joseph Holt Ingraham, Charles Sheldon, and William Ware, whose *Letters of Lucius M. Piso* (1837) is considered the first of the genre. Ingraham's *The Prince of the House of David* (1885), one of the eighty novels written by this ordained Episcopal minister, was a best-seller until the end of the century. Sheldon, a minister in Topeka, Kansas, wrote the classic *In His Steps* (1896), which sold over six million copies in twenty languages, and was available in eleven different editions in 1980.[17]

Women equaled men in the writing of successful religious novels. In Eliza B. Lee's *Naomi* (1848), Elizabeth Oakes Smith's *Bertha and Lily* (1854), and Adeline Whitney's *The Gayworthy's* (1865), a holy young daughter pits herself against a stern, puritan father and prevails. The recurrence of this theme suggests the religious conflicts between generations and genders in the pre–Civil War era.[18]

The literature and theology of homey heaven had obvious appeal for women because it indicated that eternity was their domain, as the earthly life of commerce and politics most assuredly was not. The monthly women's magazines—*Godey's, Demorest's,* and *The Lady's Friend,* for example—were full of literature of consolation, death, and such poetry as "My Saint," "Row Me Over," "The Bereaved Mother," "In Memoriam," "Dead," "Stricken,"

"Imprisoned," and "For Nellie's Mother." "Going," by Mary Tucker, is a typical piece.

> *"Good-by! A little while, good-by," he whispered,*
> *Between his kisses—softly adding then,*
> *"My little love! be strong, and brave, and patient,*
> *Loving me always, 'til I come again."*
>
> *Long are the years! Alone and unforgetting*
> *I ponder over all the words he said.*
> *When will he come again? O Heaven! have pity;*
> *Not till the grave hath given up its dead!*[19]

The 1870 volumes of *Godey's* contained seventy-one poems, of which twenty-eight (approximately forty percent) were about death. The percentage remains relatively constant for the following quarter-century.[20] The subjects of this type of poetry and fiction were ordinary people, undistinguished men, women, or children leading insignificant lives in the patriotic past or the industrial present. For these heroes, death was, ironically, life's great event: both a liberator from earthly troubles (an old idea), and the passage to the realm of reunited families and powerful, "heavenly homemakers," as Henry Ward Beecher referred to them. "Row Me Over," by Eben Rexford, expresses this:

> *Oh! The golden Sunset Ferry,*
> *How I long to cross its tide,*
> *To that fair and stately city,*
> *Where my dearest ones abide.*
> *Hasten, Boatman, ere the twilight*
> *Falls across the light of day.*
> *Row me o'er the Sunset Ferry*
> *To the city far away.*[21]

Heaven was "the city far away," a blend of the image of the New Jerusalem or Eternal City with the urban and suburban residential ethos of middle-class America.

The patriotic histories of the United States written in the post–Civil War era described events and accomplishments which women could admire but could never achieve. That sort of heroism was the prerogative of men. Religious stories about insignificant people who maintained or lost their virtue as a lesson to the reading public provided more attainable models for women. Because death was their most potent (and really only) weapon, it was interpreted as an event of glory, a beginning of even greater influence and power for women. For Elizabeth Stuart Phelps:

Death is a mood of life. It is no whim
  By which life's Giver mocks a broken heart.
Death is life's reticence. Still audible to Him
  The hushed voice, happy, speaketh on, apart.[22]

Life and afterlife were equated explicitly in literature and implicitly in the practices of embalming and dressing the corpse as if for church. The relationship is more complex than simply a "denial of death."[23] For those whose lives entailed potential control of their environment, these funeral practices signified that heaven was in fact a continuation of an important life on earth. For women, who were outside the realm of real power, these activities instead served to reduce the importance of life by characterizing it as a way-station to a better world which they would rule. The replacement of the roughly human-shaped coffin by the elaborate rectangular casket is similarly gender-distinctive in its cultural meaning. "Casket" was originally a term used to describe a container for precious materials. Women kept gems in caskets, and *The Young People's Casket* was a popular children's periodical of brief literary "gems." For men, this transition symbolized the increased value of the cargo whose soul was on its way. For women, it meant a good deal more: the eternal victory of piety, a celebration of a beginning rather than an end.

EIGHT

> The perfection of womanhood . . . is the wife and mother, the center of the family, the magnet that draws man to the domestic altar that makes him a civilized being, a social Christian. The wife is truly the light of the home.

This paean to women and motherhood appeared in *Godey's Lady's Book* in 1860. The initial two lines establish the identity between womanhood and the wifely responsibility to bear and raise children, as well as the conviction that fulfilling these responsibilities locates a woman at the center of the family. This assertion was not new in 1860, but in conjunction with the phrase "domestic altar," it signifies the dramatic change in the nature of social responsibility and political economy that was to dominate mainstream American culture in the late nineteenth century.

The joining of home and church suggested by the phrase "domestic altar" reflects the complementary movements toward secularization of the church and sanctification of the home that occurred in the latter half of the nineteenth century. The orthodoxy of seventeenth- and eighteenth-century Protestantism—which often set worldly accumulation in opposition to spiritual health—was gradually weakened by an increasing accommodation to the realities of nineteenth-century political economy. Both ministerial and lay advocates of that system drew their theoretical vigor from Adam Smith's *Wealth of Nations,* first published in 1776. Smith had argued that the general welfare of the whole populace ultimately benefited from the actions of a self-interested citizenry whose economic activity is unrestricted by state or church. He posited that the "hidden hand" of economic laws would ensure the continued ascent of developed societies like those of England or the United States. Unlike his countryman Thomas Hobbes, who in the seventeenth century had argued that individual competition produced a "war of all against all," Smith and his nineteenth-century followers were certain that their civilization would be ever-expanding, and ultimately beneficent. The "hidden hand" and the hand of God had become one.

Endowing the home with the significance of the church indicated that much of the responsibility for religious affection and nurture had been shifted away from the public space of worship to the private realm of the individual family, and particularly to the woman who resided there. In this secular environment—often enriched with ecclesiastical references—men from the competitive and unchristian world of commerce would be made "civilized." Church and home were drawn together and allied as a counterpoint to the harsh realities of the economic sector.

The division between commerce and morality and the church's relinquishing of total spiritual responsibility exemplified the rise to hegemony of the liberal capitalist world-view. As the place of work shifted from the home to the office in the city or town, so, too, the organic interrelationship of family, community, and economic activity was riven. The church had once attempted to control factors in the economic sector by such devices as the "just price," but by the mid-nineteenth century the economy operated as a theoretical antagonist to the principles of Christian behavior. In the seventeenth century, settlers in the New World had hoped to establish a series of corporate Christian communities whose light would shine out to the rest of the world like a beacon on a hill. In these settlements, the economic, political, and theological power structures (run by men) were to be united in the common quest for this end. By the middle of the nineteenth century, the beacon on the hill had become the "light of the home"; free-standing, autonomous, and run by women who had little or no direct connection with the male world of economic and political activity. This change relieved the church of responsibility for the economic affairs of its members, and cast the universe of human action into two parts: that of morality and feeling, and that of material well-being.

Yet the two orders were entwined: success in the material world was interpreted as a sign of personal virtue and vigor, a kind of morality of the marketplace. More-over, the fundamental assumption of classical nineteenth-century liberal thought—that self-interested pursuit of economic gain ultimately benefited the entire society—also contained an implicit moral justification for individual competition. So, too, the culturally designated realm of morality and feeling in the nineteenth century—the home—was totally dependent on its alleged opponent—the marketplace.

The meshing of the secular and spiritual realms of society to justify the ethos of liberal capitalism generated a powerful new sector in the circle of advisors and counselors to the populace. Ministers were joined or replaced by physicians, scientists, and corporations, adding scientific evidence and economic argument to the moral suasion and vigor of the church. Ministers to the bodily health of individuals delivered their advice in terms of moral rectitude. Physicians and scientists, like ministers, tried to control individual behavior for the greater good of society. Neurasthenia and hysteria—both diseases that ultimately came to be associated with women—were blamed on the personal failings of the afflicted. What had originally been a physical or mental condition of a minority of people ultimately was considered a general cultural condition. Characterizing society as a human organism writ large enabled apologists for classical liberal thought to account for what seemed to be evidence of cultural decline.

Since the economic and political status quo left little room for inherent contradictions and material failure, individuals were ultimately responsible for their successes or setbacks. Thus the resistance of workers to the injustices and excesses of the late-nineteenth-century economy were not seen as indicators of some weakness in the system, but as the result of some individual or collective failure among the populace. Immigrants who had not been acculturated were blamed for the discontent, but the white Anglo-Saxon Protestant majority was also faulted for allowing its mental and physical vigor to degenerate so that those newcomers were able to wrest some measure of power.

The primary responsibility for this decline belonged not to men, the prime actors in the commercial world, but to the keepers of the other segment of civilized life, their wives. Yet women who took an activist role in commercial or reform activities were censured for attempting to move out of their ordained "sphere" of "influence." The separation of the economic (male) sector from the domestic (female) sector thus placed women in the position of culpability for societal ills, but denied them access to the real means of rectifying them. Splitting rhetoric and responsibility from political and economic power meant that formal alterations in either the status of women or in issues of private morality were acceptable only if they strengthened the dominant ideological system. The two great women's political reform movements of the turn of the century—suffrage and prohibition—became law when advocates convinced opponents that maternal influence would halt the precipitous decline of WASP culture. Americans could therefore affirm and preserve the liberal creed by explaining the crises of the late nineteenth century as a personal failure—ironically, a failure of maternal influence.

Arguing that women needed political power to save men from their baser natures was more than just a shrewd political tactic. The argument was a secular descendant of the Christian idea of individual sin. It was a way by which Americans could uphold their liberal beliefs yet explain the grave cultural crises of the era. The early-nineteenth-century optimism about individual human potential that paralleled the assertion of unending economic expansion had been tempered by post–Civil War social and economic events and by the discoveries of nineteenth-century scientists. By the 1860s physicians had convinced Americans that individuals in fact had only a finite amount of energy, and that among middle-class and wealthy white Anglo-Saxon Protestants this quantum of vitality was decreasing with each generation. This was a particularly ominous development, given the huge number of immigrants entering the United States from southern and eastern Europe in the eighties and nineties. These newcomers were not only of different ethnic origin than the waves of immigrants who preceded them, but their experience in the United States would be radically different because there was no longer an American frontier. Thomas P. Gill, in 1886, and Frederick Jackson Turner, in 1893, pointed out that the nation's reserve of free land had disappeared, and was thus no longer available to absorb and transform immigrants. Fresh from the decadent cities of Europe, the "new" immigrants were unable to experience what Turnerians viewed as the ameliorative conditions of frontier life. Instead, they settled in American cities that were already crowded, transforming them into "volcanoes," full of the explosive potential of class war.

In order to reduce the pressure while upholding liberal assumptions of continuous economic expansion, turn-of-the-century critics of American society not only turned inward, they looked outward. Locating additional consumers for American products—who would not exacerbate urban congestion—underlay imperialist machinations in Latin America and the Far East, and attempts at immigration restriction. Advocates of expansion in the international economic world and limitation of immigration were able to reconcile these positions because they identified their nation and its future strength with the Anglo-Saxon ethnic heritage. Adam Smith was an Englishman.

The conviction that social problems are simply a function of personal failings has had broad ramifications. This position—basic to so much of this nation's reform activity—has not only deflected critical analysis from the core of nineteenth-century liberal economic theory, it has also enabled defenders of social or economic stasis to characterize the critic as somehow imbalanced. This tendency influences our perception of both the present and the past. In the 1950s and early 1960s, for example, historians argued that reformers—Abolitionists, Populists, and Progressives—were "status-conscious" or "paranoid" elites threatened by change in an industrializing society. In the more recent past, women struggling for equality have often encountered a similar form of response, which snidely brushes them aside as sexually frustrated social misfits. Turning questions and criticism of nineteenth-century political economy and its modern counterpart into issues of personal health perhaps explains the enduring power of that ideology, but it also reveals the flaccid moral core of our time.

NOTES

INTRODUCTION

1. *New York Herald,* May, 20, 1978, p. 6.

CHAPTER ONE. "A WOMAN'S CALLING"

1. Francis E. Willard, quoted in Gerda Lerner, ed., *The Female Experience: An American Documentary* (Indianapolis: Bobbs-Merrill Co., 1977), p. 36. This description of Willard's reaction to putting up her hair as an adolescent was recorded in her journal and later in her autobiography, *Glimpses of Fifty Years: The Autobiography of an American Woman* (Chicago: H. J. Smith & Co., 1889).

2. Florence Hall, *The Correct Thing in Good Society* (Boston: D. Estes & Co., 1888), p. 35.

3. *Godey's Lady's Book and Magazine,* vol. 61 (July 1860), pp. 80–81.

4. Ernst Lubin, *The Piano Duet* (New York: Da Capo Press, 1970), p. 4.

5. *Godey's,* vol. 81, no. 485 (November 1870), p. 429.

6. M. S. Logan, *The Home Manual* (Chicago: H. J. Smith & Co., 1889), p. 79.

7. *Godey's,* vol. 80, no. 478 (April 1870), p. 395.

8. *The Woman's Home Companion,* November 1899, p. 43.

9. E. S. Turner, *A History of Courting* (London: M. Joseph, 1954), p. 183. Turner quotes from Frederick B. Meyer, *Love, Courtship and Marriage* (1899): "I should commend the man who consulted the family doctor of the girl to whom he was intending to propose, lest there should be any insanity or heredity taint in her family; . . . and surely the father of any girl or any woman for herself should be at liberty before giving the final answer to ask of any young man the name of some physician who would be able to speak for him and his."

10. *Godey's,* vol. 80, no. 477 (March 1870), p. 299.

11. *Godey's,* vol. 81, no. 486 (December 1870), pp. 541–43.

12. *Demorest's Monthly Magazine,* vol. 14, no. 5 (May 1878), p. 282; *Demorest's,* vol. 14, no. 11 (November 1878), p. 620; *Godey's,* vol. 81, no. 481 (July 1870), p. 97.

13. Quoted in Lerner, *Female Experience,* p. 52.

14. *Godey's,* vol. 80, no. 477 (March 1870), p. 299.

15. Grace H. Dodge, *A Bundle of Letters* (New York: Funk & Wagnalls, 1887), pp. 39, 104.

16. S. L. Louis, *Decorum* (New York: Union Publishing House, 1882), p. 192.

17. Quoted in John S. Haller and Robin M. Haller, *The Physician and Sexuality in Victorian America* (Urbana: University of Illinois Press, 1974), p. 110.

18. Jean E. Friedman and William G. Shade, *Our American Sisters* (Boston: Little, Brown & Co., 1973), p. 294, and Theodore K. Rabb and Robert Rotberg, *The Family in History* (New York: Harper & Row, 1971), pp. 88–90. See also Philip Greven, Jr., *Four Generations* (Ithaca, N.Y.: Cornell University Press, 1970), p. 208.

19. *The Young People's Mirror and American Family Visitor* (1 October 1849), p. 113; D. Dora Nickerson, "Old Maids," *The Household,* vol. 7, no. 8 (August 1874), p. 189.

20. Quoted in Lerner, *Female Experience,* pp. 24–25.

21. Nancy Cott, *Roots of Bitterness* (New York: E. P. Dutton & Co., 1972), p. 116; Samuel K. Jennings, *The Married Lady's Companion, or Poor Man's Friend,* rev. 2nd ed. (New York: Harper & Brothers, 1898), pp. 61–68.

22. William Tegg, *The Knot Tied* (1877; reprint ed., Detroit, Mich.: Singing Tree Press, 1970), p. 298.

23. Logan, *Home Manual,* p. 41.

24. Diaries of Almira D. MacDonald, 26 May 1909, 16–17 March 1882, 11 June 1909, 12 June 1909, Margaret Woodbury Strong Museum, Rochester, N.Y.

25. *Godey's,* vol. 80, no. 477 (March 1870), p. 295; *Godey's,* vol. 86, no. 511 (January 1873), p. 96.

26. Diaries of Almira MacDonald, 28 June 1909.

27. Interview with Mary Wilcox DeMund, 7 June 1979, Rochester, N.Y.; interview with John H. Earl, October 1977, Bloomfield, N.J. In 1870 *Godey's* suggested pearl-gray silk for the bride who was "no longer young," that is, over the age of thirty. Brides with limited means were urged to marry in a traveling dress and hat rather than spend money wastefully on a gown that would be of limited service after the ceremony. The recommended dress was of poplin, "cloth" (wool) or serge, and the hat of felt or velvet, matching the color of the dress. Although particular colors were not specified for the traveling outfit, "all conspicuous colors, trimmings, and everything that will proclaim bridehood should always be avoided." *Godey's,* vol. 80, no. 476 (February 1870), p. 206.

28. Diaries of Almira MacDonald, 8 March 1881; interview with Mary Wilcox DeMund, 7 June 1979.

29. W. D. Howells, *Their Wedding Journey* (Boston: Houghton Mifflin Co., 1888), p. 8; interview with Mary Wilcox DeMund, 21 February 1980, Rochester, N.Y. (family tradition does not tell us whether the newlyweds' subterfuge was successful or not); Florence Hartley, *The Ladies' Book of Etiquette and Manual of Politeness* (Boston: G. W. Cottrell, 1860), p. 259.

30. On January 24, 1871, Almira MacDonald noted in her diary: "At 7½ Husband & I rode to Rev. Richardsons on Poultney St. who gave a reception to their oldest-son Edward married seven weeks ago to Mary McLaren."

31. *The Woman's Home Companion,* November 1899, p. 24.

32. *The Household,* vol. 15, no. 10 (October 1882), p. 290.

CHAPTER TWO. MADONNA IN THE NURSERY

1. "Timothy Titcomb" [Josiah Gilbert Holland], *Titcomb's Letters to Young People, Single and Married* (New York: Charles Scribner, 1858), pp. 200–1.

2. Ibid., p. 201; Mrs. E. G. Cook, M.D., "Sanitar-ian," *Demorest's Monthly Magazine,* vol. 23, no. 8 (June 1887), p. 500; *Godey's Lady's Book and Magazine,* vol. 60 (December 1860), pp. 529–30.

3. H. S. Pomeroy, *Ethics of Marriage* (New York: Funk & Wagnalls, 1888).

4. See Carroll Smith-Rosenberg, "Puberty to Menopause: The Cycle of Femininity in Nineteenth-Century America," in Mary Hartman and Lois Banner, eds., *Clio's Consciousness Raised* (New York: Harper & Row, 1974), pp. 23–37.

5. *Historical Statistics of the United States* (Washington, D.C.: U.S. Government Printing Office, 1976), p. 49; [Holland], *Titcomb's Letters,* pp. 53–54.

6. Daniel Scott-Smith, "Family Limitation, Sexual Control, and Domestic Feminism in Victorian America," in Hartman and Banner, eds., *Clio's Consciousness Raised,* pp. 121–22; see also Cook, "Sanitarian," p. 500.

7. Carroll Smith-Rosenberg and Charles Rosenberg, "The Female Animal: Medical and Biological Views of Woman and Her Role in Nineteenth-Century America," *Journal of American History,* vol. 60, no. 2 (September 1973), pp. 332–56.

8. [Holland], *Titcomb's Letters,* p. 202.

9. A. M. Mauriceau, *The Married Woman's Private Medical Companion* (New York: Joseph Trow, 1855), pp. 142–43. Mauriceau's book was first published in 1847 and remained in print throughout the century. A prototype for the modern diaphragm was patented in 1846 by J. B. Beers, who called it "the Wife's Protector."

10. [Holland], *Titcomb's Letters,* p. 203; Mary Wood-Allen, *What a Young Woman Ought to Know* (Philadelphia: Vir Publishing Co., 1905), p. 250.

11. Wood-Allen, *What a Young Woman Ought to Know,* p. 114.

12. Susan Hooker to Alcesta Huntington, 19 August

1872, Huntington-Hooker Papers, University of Rochester, Rochester, N.Y.

13. Emma Drake, *What a Young Wife Ought to Know* (Philadelphia: Vir Publishing Co., 1908), pp. 121, 119.

14. "Maternity," *The Household,* vol. 12, no. 4 (April 1879), p. 79.

15. Regina Morantz and Sue Zschoche, "Professionalism, Feminism and Gender Roles: A Comparative Study of Nineteenth Century Medical Therapeutics," *Journal of American History,* vol. 67, no. 3 (December 1980), pp. 568–88.

16. Sophia North, "My Child," *Godey's,* vol. 60 (August 1860), pp. 124–26.

17. Benjamin Wadsworth, *The Nature of Early Piety* (Boston: n.p., 1721), quoted in Stanley Schultz, *The Culture Factory* (New York: Oxford University Press, 1973), p. 48. For a provocative study of childrearing in colonial America, see Philip Greven, *The Protestant Temperament* (New York: Alfred A. Knopf, 1980).

18. Jacob Abbott, *Gentle Measures in the Management and Training of Children.* (New York: Harper & Brothers, 1871), p. 11.

19. Bernard Wishy, *The Child and the Republic* (Philadelphia: University of Pennsylvania Press, 1969), p. 111.

20. Kate Taylor to Annjenett Huntington, 10 December 1876, Huntington-Hooker Papers; "Willie's Mamma" and "Window Greenery," *Hearth and Home,* vol. 11, no. 10 (26 February 1870). p. 155.

21. "Weatherproof Homes," *The Household,* vol. 12, no. 4 (April 1879), p. 73.

22. Michael Kammen, *A Season of Youth* (New York: Alfred A. Knopf, 1978); George Forgie, *Patricide in the House Divided* (New York: W. W. Norton & Co., 1979); Fred Somkin, *Unquiet Eagle: Memory and Desire in the Idea of American Freedom, 1815–1860* (Ithaca, N.Y.: Cornell University Press, 1967).

23. J. Stainback Wilson, M.D., "Mothers Should Nurse Their Children," *Godey's,* vol. 61 (July 1860), pp. 80–81.

24. J. Stainback Wilson, M.D., "Diet and Drinks of Nursing Women," *Godey's,* vol. 61 (December 1860), p. 558.

25. Moses T. Runnells, "Physical Degeneracy of American Women," *Medical Era,* vol. 3 (1886), p. 298.

26. J. N. Hanaford, M.D., "The Care of Infants," *The Household,* vol. 7, no. 2 (February 1874), p. 30; Charles P. Uhle, M.D., "Infants' Food," *Godey's,* vol. 80, no. 479 (May 1870), pp. 479–80; J. Stainback Wilson, M.D., "Raising Children by Hand," *Godey's,* vol. 61 (August 1860), pp. 175–76. See also "Take Care of the Babies," *The Household,* vol. 12, no. 10 (October 1879), p. 223; "Artificial Nursing," *Good Housekeeping,* vol. 9, no. 2 (25 May 1889), p. 38.

27. Mellin's Food Company, *Diet After Weaning* (Boston, 1905), unpaged; Kate Taylor to Alcesta Huntington, 1 June 1880, Huntington-Hooker Papers.

28. "Food for Infants," *The Household,* vol. 12, no. 1 (January 1879), p. 8.

29. Mrs. Henry N. Stone, "Information Concerning the Care of Infants and Children," *The Household,* vol. 13, no. 8 (August 1880), p. 189. The advertisement appears on p. 192.

30. Mellin's, *Diet After Weaning.*

31. Mrs. E. G. Cook, M.D., "Sanitarian," *Demorest's,* vol. 23, no. 11 (September 1887), p. 716.

32. We sometimes forget that temperance, for all the melodrama of its advocates, became a law by constitutional amendment. Thus, we run the risk of neglecting important evidence about the conduct of life in the late nineteenth century if we pass over temperance writers in favor of those thinkers who more accurately represent concerns of the middle and late twentieth century.

33. *The Bazar-Book of Decorum* (New York: Harper & Brothers, 1870), p. 78.

34. Abba Gould Woolson, ed., *Dress-Reform* (Boston: Roberts Brothers, 1874), p. 26. See also "Some Hints on the Management of Children," *Godey's,* vol. 92, no. 549 (March 1876), p. 283.

35. *Good Housekeeping,* vol. 8, no. 9 (2 March 1889), inside front cover.

36. *Bazar-Book of Decorum,* p. 59.

37. *The Ladies' Guide to True Politeness and Perfect Manners, or Miss Leslie's Behavior Book* (Philadelphia: T. B. Peterson & Brothers, 1864) pp. 286–87.

38. "The Tepid Bath," *Godey's,* vol. 80, no. 481 (July 1870), p. 569.

39. "On the Education of Children," *Godey's,* vol. 81, no. 485 (November 1870), p. 453; "The Education of Children," *Godey's,* vol. 92, no. 548 (February 1876), p. 157.

40. "Manual Training in the Household," *Good Housekeeping,* vol. 8, no. 6 (19 January 1889), p. 126.

41. Harvey Newcomb, *How to Be a Man* (Boston: Gould & Lincoln, 1851), p. 37; [Holland], *Titcomb's Letters,* pp. 224–25; Catherine Beecher, *Beecher's Domestic Economy* (New York: Harper & Brothers, 1858), pp. 227, 224 (Beecher's *Treatise on Domestic Economy* went through several editions after its first publication in 1847); Newcomb, *How to Be a Man,* p. 119; Timothy Shay Arthur, *The True Path and How to Walk Therein* (Rochester, N.Y.: E. Darrow & Brother, 1856), p. 39; "Earnest Words with Parents," *The Household,* vol. 7, no. 8 (August 1874), p. 175. See also Mrs. E. G. Cook, M.D., "Children's Rights," *Demorest's,* vol. 23, no. 10 (August 1887), p. 647. Cook stated that "children have the right to employment . . . to be taught politeness and reverence . . . [and] obedience."

42. "Occupation of Children," *Godey's,* vol. 81, no. 485 (November 1870), p. 483; Mellin's, *Diet After Weaning.*

43. Mary Barr Munroe, "Table Etiquette," *Good Housekeeping,* vol. 9, no. 2 (25 May 1889), pp. 36–37. See also "Table Manners," *The Household,* vol. 14, no. 4 (April 1881), p. 80, for a harangue on eating with one's knife, and "Let the Children Alone," *Godey's,* vol. 81, no. 483 (September 1870), p. 285.

44. "Earnest Words with Parents," *The Household,* vol. 7, no. 8 (August 1874), p. 175; Beecher, *Treatise on Domestic Economy,* p. 143; "Educator" and "Courtesy in Childhood," *The Household,* vol. 12, no. 4 (April 1879), p. 79.

45. H. Maria George, "Remarks on Housekeeping," *The Household,* vol. 13, no. 3 (March 1880), p. 60; [John H. Young], *Our Deportment* (Detroit, Mich.: F. B. Dickerson, 1879), pp. 214 ff.

46. *Miss Leslie's Behavior Book,* p. 295.

47. Jacob Abbott, *The Rollo Code* (Boston: W. J. Reynolds & Co., 1841), and *Rollo on the Atlantic* (Boston: Brown, Taggard & Chase, 1858).

48. See Bernard Wishy, *The Child and the Republic,* pp. 81–93.

49. Palmer Cox, *The Brownies, Their Book* (New York: Century Co., 1887).

50. *Godey's,* vol. 60 (July 1860), p. 79; Thomas G. Gentry, "A Mother's Worth," *Godey's,* vol. 87, no. 522 (December 1873), p. 518.

51. Elizabeth Cady Stanton, "The Matriarchate, or, Mother-Age," in *The Transactions of the National Council of Women of the United States* (Washington, D.C.: Government Printing Office, 1891), pp. 222, 224.

52. [Holland], *Titcomb's Letters,* pp. 158, 150–51, 153.

53. Eliza B. Duffey, *The Relations of the Sexes* (New York, 1876), p. 219, quoted in John S. Haller and Robin M. Haller, *The Physician and Sexuality in Victorian America* (Urbana: University of Illinois Press, 1974), pp. 100–1.

CHAPTER THREE. CLEANLINESS AND GODLINESS

1. "Letters to the Household," *The Household,* vol. 15, no. 2 (February 1882), p. 50.

2. Shirley F. Murphy, *Our Homes and How to Make Them Healthy* (London: Cassell & Co., 1883), p. 312.

3. Mrs. M. H. Cornelius, *The Young Housekeeper's Friend* (Boston: Taggard & Thompson, 1868), p. 9.

4. "Ladies in Agricultural Colleges," *Godey's La-*

dy's Book and Magazine, vol. 80, no. 476 (February 1870), p. 190.

5. Cornelius, *Young Housekeeper's Friend,* p. 18.

6. Diaries of Almira D. MacDonald, 1856–1885, Margaret Woodbury Strong Museum, Rochester, N.Y.

7. William G. Panschar, *Baking in America,* vol. 1, *Economic Development* (Evanston, Ill.: Northwestern University Press, 1956), p. 34.

8. "Gypsey Traine" and "Baking Day," *The Household,* vol. 7, no. 7 (July 1874), p. 156; "To Make Bread," *The Household,* vol. 12, no. 10 (October 1879), p. 229.

9. Advertisement for the Sterling Range, *The Jury,* vol. 1, no. 1 (2 November 1889), p. 13; Susan Hooker to Alcesta Huntington, 4 February 1886, Huntington-Hooker Papers, University of Rochester, Rochester, N.Y.

10. Diaries of Almira MacDonald, 1870.

11. Agnes B. Ormsbee, "Jelly-Making," *Good Housekeeping,* vol. 9, no. 7 (3 August 1889), p. 151.

12. Agnes B. Ormsbee, "Canning Fruit," *Good Housekeeping,* vol. 9, no. 5 (6 July 1889), p. 108.

13. "Canned Fruits and Vegetables," *The Household,* vol. 14, no. 8 (August 1881), p. 181; Ormsbee, "Canning Fruit," p. 108.

14. *Sears Roebuck Catalog,* 1902, p. 573. A crank-driven combination parer, corer, and slicer could be purchased from Sears Roebuck for thirty-nine cents in 1902. The same catalog advertised a "Rotary Knife, Family Peach and Apple Parer" for ninety-eight cents.

15. Alcesta Huntington to Annjenett Huntington, 10 December 1867, Huntington-Hooker Papers.

16. "Rosella Rice," "At Our Home," *The Household,* vol. 12, no. 2 (February 1879), p. 36.

17. Leonore Glenn, "Jottings Here and There," *The Household,* vol. 12, no. 2 (February 1879), p. 36.

18. *Sears Roebuck Catalog,* 1902, p. 573.

19. Elizabeth F. Holt, *From Attic to Cellar* (Salem, Mass: The Salem Press, 1892), pp. 1, 3–5, 6–7.

20. Alcesta Huntington to Annjenett Huntington, 1 April 1868, Huntington-Hooker Papers; Alcesta Huntington to Kate Taylor, 5 January 1883, Huntington-Hooker Papers; Journal of Harriet T. Bailie, 14 August 1893, Sophia Smith Collection, Smith College Library, Northampton, Mass.

21. I am not able to explain the constancy of pay scales for visiting domestic service between 1865 and 1900. The value of currency fluctuated during this period, and the two-dollar rate seems to be almost a folk tradition, apart from the vagaries of the marketplace.

22. Cornelius, *Young Housekeeper's Friend,* pp. 230–31. Elizabeth F. Holt recommended a similar method in 1892 in *From Attic to Cellar,* p. 84. See also Annie Wade, "How to Lighten the Work of Wash-day," *Good Housekeeping,* vol. 8, no. 10 (16 March 1889), pp. 232–33.

23. Barbara Brandt, "Washing Day," *The Household,* vol. 7, no. 10 (October 1874), p. 228; "Large and Small Washings," *The Household,* vol. 7, no. 11 (November 1874), p. 253.

24. *Sears Roebuck Catalog,* 1902, p. 569.

25. "Ironing," *Godey's,* vol. 93, no. 556 (October 1876), p. 376. The Huntington sisters hired someone to iron when they were between servants. Alcesta wrote her mother in 1868 that "Mrs. Sanger had been ironing for us today. Still no girl" (Alcesta Huntington to Annjenett Huntington, 13 February 1868, Huntington-Hooker Papers). Ten years later they continued to send out laundry every two weeks. It cost them two dollars (Susan Hooker to Annjenett Huntington, 4 March 1878).

26. Diaries of Almira MacDonald 3 December 1870. Every manuscript source closely investigated over time held to this pattern. The major sources are: Diaries of Mrs. E. C. Smith, 1883–85; Diaries of Carrie T. Lyon, 1870–1910; Letters of Susan Hooker, 1865–1900; Letters of Alcesta Huntington, 1865–1900: Letters of Annjenett Huntington, 1865–1900; Letters of Kate Taylor,

1865–1900; Letters of Carrie Jessup, 1865–1900; Diaries of Cornelia B. Ellwanger, 1871–77; Diary of A. Bradner, 1885; Diary of Caroline R. Hopkins, 1883; Diaries of Julia R. Irving, 1870–74; Diaries of Harriet E. Hamilton, 1889, 1901; all in the University of Rochester Libraries, Rochester, N.Y. Another source, in addition to the MacDonald diaries, is Maude Motley's diaries 1896–1900, in the collection of the Margaret Woodbury Strong Museum, Rochester, N.Y.

27. J. H. J. "Sweeping Day," *The Household,* vol. 13, no. 12 (December 1880), pp. 245–75. This article states that Friday is the general sweeping day, although the journals and diaries examined suggest no clear predominance of either Friday or Saturday.

28. Martha B. Bruere, "The New Home-Making," *Outlook,* vol. 100 (16 March 1912), p. 592.

29. Diaries of Mrs. E. Clayton Smith, 1883, University of Rochester.

30. Diaries of Almira MacDonald, 1885, 1870.

31. Susan Hooker to Annjenett Huntington, 8 December 1878, Huntington-Hooker Papers.

32. Diary of Lydia Maria Child (1864), quoted in Gerda Lerner, ed., *The Female Experience: An American Documentary* (Indianapolis: Bobbs-Merrill Co., 1977), pp. 125–26. On August 16, 1869, Almira MacDonald noted in her diary that she was "busy fixing carpet stools and cushioning chairs." On October 10 of the following year she "mended the dining room carpet." Ritual meals and celebrations were another part of the yearly cycle of work. Servants, if they were present in the household, may have performed some of the mundane cooking chores associated with Thanksgiving and Christmas, but the special sauces and pastries were prepared by the woman who ran the house. On Tuesday, November 22, 1870, MacDonald noted that she made "mincemeat and gold and silver cake," on Wednesday "baked mincemeat pies and made the stuffing for the turkey." She changed her baking schedule for Christmas, which fell on a Sunday that year, baking chocolate, "cornstarch cakes, mince pies" on Friday, December 23. Saturday was reserved for preparing the remainder of the meal since her one domestic helper, a cook, had gone home for Christmas. The pattern of activity was constant until MacDonald no longer cooked. (She lived with her daughter by 1900.)

33. "An Old Dress Made Over," *The Household,* vol. 12, no. 1 (January 1879), p. 4 (for a reference to paper patterns, see Allie E. Whittaker, "Cutting and Making," *The Household,* vol. 14, no. 8 [August 1881], p. 172); Annjenett Huntington to Alcesta Huntington, 10 December 1868, Huntington-Hooker Papers.

34. Alcesta Huntington to Annjenett Huntington, 12 March 1868, Huntington-Hooker Papers; Annjenett Huntington to Alcesta Huntington, 13 December 1868; Susan Hooker to Annjenett Huntington, 22 March 1868.

35. Diary of Almira MacDonald, 1870.

36. "The Queen of Inventions—The Sewing Machine," *Godey's,* vol. 61 (July 1860), pp. 77, 78.

37. "Sewing Machine Clubs," *Godey's,* vol. 61 (September 1860), p. 271 (in 1902 Sears Roebuck offered the "High Grade Minnesota Machine" for twenty-three dollars); "The Sewing Machine and Its Merits," *Godey's,* vol. 61 (October 1860), p. 369.

38. "Sewing Machine Clubs," *Godey's,* p. 271.

39. Ibid, p. 271.

40. "The Queen of Inventions," *Godey's,* p. 78; Antoinette Brown Blackwell, "The Relation of Women's Work in the Household to the Work Outside," in *Papers and Letters Presented at the First Women's Congress of the Association for the Advancement of Woman* (New York: Harper & Brothers, 1874), p. 181; Abba Gould Woolson, ed., *Dress-Reform* (Boston: Roberts Brothers, 1874), pp. 93–94.

41. Mrs. Hopkinson, "Some Thoughts on the Completed Century," *Godey's,* vol. 92, no. 547 (January 1876), p. 33.

42. Hazel Wylde, "The Art of Housekeeping," *The Household,* vol. 13, no. 3 (March 1880), p. 60.

43. J. N. Hanaford, M.D., "Women's Work," *The Household,* vol. 14, no. 3 (March 1881), p. 162; see also H. Maria George, "Remarks on House-keeping," *The Household,* vol. 13, no. 3 (March 1880), p. 60.

44. See Christopher Monkhouse, "The Spinning Wheel as Artifact, Symbol, and Source of Design," in Kenneth L. Ames, ed., *Nineteenth-Century Furniture* (Watkins Glen, N.Y.: American Life Foundation, forthcoming); see also Harvey Green, "The Ironies of Style, Complexities and Traditions in American Decorative Arts, 1850–1900," in *Nineteenth-Century Furniture.*

45. Women on the frontier or on isolated rural farms had some assistance from their children, if they had any. But they were expected to perform some of the farm chores as well. Many were also responsible for the family garden. One might surmise, then, that the rural woman's fate was a grim one. Evidence suggests that farm life was isolated and incredibly harsh by our standards. See Frank Blackmar, "The Smoky Pilgrims," *American Journal of Sociology,* vol. 2, no. 4 (January 1897). A controversial and significant book is Michael Lesy, *Wisconsin Death Trip* (New York: Pantheon Books, 1973). For a counterpoint to Lesy's vision, see George Talbot et al., *At Home: Domestic Life in the Post-Centennial Era* (Madison: State Historical Society of Wisconsin, 1976). A good example of how a moderately successful farm operated can be found in Susan Hooker's letter of 1886 to her mother, Annjenett Huntington: "The stock is doing nicely under Harry's efforts. Bert [21 years] milks, Lon [17] tends to the furnace and cellar, and Harry [14] and Paul [11] and Willard [10] do most of the chores. The chickens are very contented and happy but utterly refuse to lay an egg" (Huntington-Hooker Papers).

46. Kate Taylor to Annjenett Huntington, 23 May 1880, Huntington-Hooker Papers; Carolyn T. Lyon to Mary Lovelace, 1901, Carolyn T. Lyon Papers.

47. Susan Hooker to Annjenett Huntington, 2 February 1869, Huntington-Hooker Papers. On April 19, 1878, Almira MacDonald noted in her diary that she "helped the new girl put down the carpet."

48. David Katzman, *Seven Days a Week: Woman and Domestic Service in Industrializing America* (New York: Oxford University Press, 1978), pp. 44–46; *Tenth Census: 1880,* vol. 1, passim; *Twelfth Census: 1900, Population,* vol. 2, pt. 2, pp. clxi–clxiv, *Occupations,* passim; *Fourteenth Census: 1920, Population,* vol. 3, pp. 40–46, *Occupations,* passim; Gwendolyn Wright, *Moralism and the Model Home* (Chicago: University of Chicago Press, 1980), p. 36.

49. "Timothy Titcomb" [Josiah Gilbert Holland], *Titcomb's Letters to Young People, Single and Married* (New York: Charles Scribner, 1858), p. 216; Catherine Beecher, *Miss Beecher's Domestic Receipt Book* (New York: Harper & Brothers, 1846), p. 281.

50. Philip Greven, *Four Generations* (Ithaca, N.Y.: Cornell University Press, 1970). See also David Rothman, *The Discovery of the Asylum* (Boston: Little, Brown & Co., 1971), pp. 69–71; and James C. Malin, *The Contriving Brain and the Skillful Hand in United States History* (Lawrence: University of Kansas Press, 1955).

51. Alcesta Huntington to Kate Taylor, 5 January 1883, Huntington-Hooker Papers; Susan Hooker to Alcesta Huntington, 22 January 1883; Susan Hooker to Alcesta Huntington, 2 February 1883.

52. Alcesta Huntington to Annjenett Huntington, 5 February 1868, Huntington-Hooker Papers.

53. Diaries of Almira MacDonald, 23 February 1885.

54. Kate Taylor to Annjenett Huntington, 3 October 1880, Huntington-Hooker Papers; Carrie Jessup to Susan Hooker, 13 May 1888.

55. [Holland], *Titcomb's Letters,* pp. 290–91.

56. Gail Laughlin, "Domestic Service," *Report of the*

Industrial Commission, vol. 14 (Washington, D.C.: Government Printing Office, 1901), p. 759.

57. Virginia Y. McLaughlin, "Patterns of Work and Family Organization: Buffalo's Italians," *Journal of Interdisciplinary History,* vol. 2 (Autumn 1971), pp. 299–314; Kate Taylor to Annjenett Huntington, 25 September 1880, Huntington-Hooker Papers.

CHAPTER FOUR. PIANO IN THE PARLOR

1. Mary Gay Humphreys, "House Decoration and Furnishing," in *The House and Home, A Practical Book,* vol. 2 (New York: Charles Scribner's Sons, 1896), p. 113.

2. See Gwendolyn Wright, *Moralism and the Model Home* (Chicago: University of Chicago Press, 1980), p. 13.

3. Janet Ruutz-Rees, *Home Decoration* (New York: D. Appleton & Co., 1881), pp. 87, 90.

4. Diaries of Almira D. MacDonald, 11 October 1895, Margaret Woodbury Strong Museum, Rochester, N.Y.

5. Ruutz-Rees, *Home Decoration,* p. 110.

6. *The Household,* vol. 15, no. 7 (July 1882), p. 221; Humphreys, "House Decoration and Furnishing," p. 123.

7. Mrs. E. G. Cook, M.D., "The Necessity for Ventilation," *Demorest's Monthly Magazine,* vol. 23, no. 12 (October 1887), p. 775; Anna Holyoke, "Wood Carpeting," *The Household,* vol. 7, no. 10 (October 1874), p. 218.

8. Robert W. Edis, "Internal Decoration," in Shirley F. Murphy, ed., *Our Homes and How to Make Them Healthy* (London: Cassell & Co., 1883), p. 313; Humphreys, "House Decoration and Furnishing," p. 147.

9. Mary Wood-Allen, *What a Young Woman Ought to Know* (Philadelphia: Vir Publishing Co., 1905), p. 80.

10. Helen Churchill Candee, "House Building," in *The House and Home,* vol. 2, p. 156.

11. *The Household,* vol. 14, no. 1 (January 1881), p. 5.

12. *The Household,* vol. 15, no. 7 (July 1882), p.

221; Diaries of Almira MacDonald, 1870, 1871, 1881.

13. *Catalog of the Publications of Louis Prang and Co., Fine Art Publishers* (Boston, 1883), pp. 3, 6, 27.

14. Ibid.; *Catalog of Consolidated Portrait and Frame Co.* (Chicago, 1904), pp. 50–56, 9.

15. David Barquist, "Art Reproductions in the Victorian Home, 1850–1900," unpublished manuscript, University of Delaware, Winterthur Program in Early American Culture, 1979.

16. Kenneth L. Ames, "Material Culture as Non-Verbal Communication," *Journal of American Culture,* vol. 3, no. 4 (Winter 1980), pp. 619–41.

17. Almon C. Varney, *Our Homes and Their Adornments* (Detroit: J. C. Chilton & Co., 1882), p. 259.

CHAPTER FIVE. THE TEMPLE OF VIRTUE

1. Mary Wood-Allen, *What a Young Woman Ought to Know,* (Philadelphia: Vir Publishing Co., 1905), p. 23.

2. For a suggestive study of Catherine Beecher and her work, see Katherine Kish Sklar, *Catherine Beecher* (New Haven, Conn.: Yale University Press, 1973). See also Timothy Shay Arthur, *Advice to Young Ladies* (Boston: Phillips, Sampson, 1853); T. S. Arthur, *The True Path and How to Walk Therein* (Rochester, N.Y.: E. Darrow & Brother, 1856); Marion Kirkland Reid, *Woman: Her Education and Influence* (New York: Fowlers & Wells, 1848); J. M. Austin, *Golden Steps for Youth of Both Sexes* (Auburn, N.Y.: Derby, Miller & Co., 1852); "Timothy Titcomb" [Josiah Gilbert Holland], *Titcomb's Letters to Young People, Single and Married* (New York: Charles Scribner, 1858); Henry Ward Beecher, *Beecher's Lectures to Young Men* (Salem, Mass.: Brooks, 1845); Harvey Newcomb, *How to Be a Woman* (Salem, Mass.: The Salem Press, 1851).

3. "New Diseases," *Godey's Lady's Book and*

Magazine, vol. 61 (August 1860), p. 190; *Godey's,* vol. 60 (May 1860), p. 467.

4. J. H. Kellogg, *Household Manual of Domestic Hygiene, Food and Diet* (Battle Creek, Mich.: Good Health Publishing Co., 1882), pp. 120–23; "Sanitarian," *Demorest's Monthly Magazine,* vol. 23, no. 7 (May 1887), p. 438.

5. *The Bazar-Book of Decorum* (New York: Harper & Brothers, 1870), pp. 43, 20–21. For a provocative and engaging inquiry into the uses of disease, see Susan Sontag, *Illness as Metaphor* (New York: Farrar, Strauss & Giroux, 1979).

6. "How to Lengthen Life," *The Household,* vol. 7, no. 8 (August 1874), p. 177.

7. John Wiltbank, "Introductory Lesson for the Session 1853–1854," *Philadelphia College of Medicine* (Philadelphia: Philadelphia College of Medicine, 1854), p. 7.

8. Carroll Smith-Rosenberg, "Puberty to Menopause: The Cycle of Femininity in Nineteenth-Century America," in Mary Hartman and Lois Banner, eds., *Clio's Consciousness Raised* (New York: Harper & Row, 1974), p. 26.

9. S. Weir Mitchell, *Wear and Tear, or Hints for the Over-Worked* (Philadelphia: J. B. Lippincott Co., 1887), pp. 35–36; "Sanitarian," *Demorest's,* vol. 23, no. 8 (June 1887), p. 499. See also Carroll Smith-Rosenberg and Charles Rosenberg, "The Female Animal: Medical and Biological Views of Woman and Her Role in Nineteenth-Century America," *Journal of American History,* vol. 60, no. 2 (September 1973), pp. 332–56.

10. Wood-Allen, *What a Young Woman Ought to Know,* pp. 123–24; Orson S. Fowler, *Creative and Sexual Science: Or Manhood, Womanhood, and their Mutual Interrelations: . . . Sexual Impairments. Restored, Male Vigor and Female Health and Beauty Perpetuated and Augmented, etc. as Taught by Phrenology and Physiology* (New York: Physical Culture Publishing Co., 1870), p. 891. See also Dee Garrison, "Immoral Fiction in the Late Victorian Library," *American Quarterly,* vol. 28 (Spring 1976), pp. 71–89.

11. Fowler, *Creative and Sexual Science,* p. 867; Wood-Allen, *What a Young Woman Ought to Know,* p. 119.

12. Diaries of Almira D. MacDonald, 1885, Margaret Woodbury Strong Museum, Rochester, N.Y.

13. Carroll Smith-Rosenberg, "Puberty to Menopause," p. 27.

14. Emma F. Drake, *What a Woman of Forty-Five Ought to Know* (Philadelphia: Vir Publishing Co., 1902), p. 39.

15. Michel Foucault, *Madness and Civilization* (New York: Random House, 1973) and *Discipline and Punish* (New York: Random House, 1979). See also Karen Horney, *Feminine Psychology* (New York: W. W. Norton & Co., 1967). Horney convincingly argued that men fear women, and respond to that fear by either denigrating them, especially their genitals, or overcompensate for these fears by elevating nonsexual areas to positions of high esteem.

16. *Bazar-Book of Decorum,* p. 67.

17. Orson S. Fowler, *Tight-Lacing, Founded on Physiology and Phrenology; or, the Evils Inflicted on Mind and Body by Compressing the Organs of Life, Thereby Retarding and Enfeebling the Vital Functions* (New York: O. S. Fowler, 1846), p. 10. See also Antoinette Brown Blackwell, "The Relation of Women's Work in the Household to the Work Outside," *Papers and Letters Presented at the First Women's Congress of the Association for the Advancement of Women* (New York, 1874), p. 180.

18. Fowler, *Tight-Lacing,* pp. 12–13; Moses T. Runnells, "Physical Degeneracy of American Women," *Medical Era,* vol. 3 (1886), p. 301.

19. See John S. Haller and Robin M. Haller, *The Physician and Sexuality in Victorian America* (Urbana: University of Illinois Press, 1974), pp. 168–69.

20. A. M. Mauriceau, *The Married Woman's Private Medical Companion* (New York: Joseph Trow, 1855), p. 164; see also Charles Graham Can-

naday, "The Relation of Tight Lacing to Uterine Development and Abdominal Pelvic Disease," *American Gynecological and Obstetrical Journal,* vol. 5 (1894), pp. 636–37.

21. Shepard and Dudley, *Trade Catalog* (New York, c. 1880).

22. Abba Gould Woolson, ed., *Dress-Reform* (Boston: Roberts Brothers, 1874), pp. 42, 78, 54, xiv, ix, 85.

23. F. M. S., "A Possible Improvement," *The Household,* vol. 7, no. 9 (September 1874), p. 197; "Aida," "Dress Reform," *The Household,* vol. 12, no. 6 (June 1879), p. 124; Woolson, *Dress-Reform,* p. 11.

24. "Aida," "Dress Reform," p. 124; Woolson, *Dress-Reform,* p. 11.

25. Woolson, *Dress-Reform,* p. 75; Charles P. Uhle, M.D., "Corns," *Godey's,* vol. 80, no. 477 (March 1870), pp. 288–89.

26. "Aida," "Dress Reform," p. 124; John H. Kellogg, *Ladies Guide in Health and Disease: Girlhood, Maidenhood, Wifehood, Motherhood* (Des Moines, Iowa: W. D. Condit & Co., 1883), p. 132.

27. Thorstein Veblen, "The Economic Theory of Women's Dress," *Popular Science Monthly,* vol. 55 (1894), pp. 198–203. Veblen's more lengthy and in some ways more difficult and penetrating book, *The Theory of the Leisure Class* (New York: A. M. Kelly, 1899) is often cited as being brilliant and largely unread. That his article appeared in one of the most significant and popular journals of the era indicates not only a greater audience for his work, but also that the ideas contained in the essay were perhaps more easily comprehended and less shocking than some critics would have us believe.

28. See Howard Mumford Jones, *The Age of Energy* (New York: Viking Press, 1970), chap. 6, esp. pp. 259–300.

29. Two provocative articles on the structure of homes and their meaning in mid-nineteenth-century America are: Clifford Clark, Jr., "Domestic Architecture as an Index to Social History: The Romantic Revival and the Cult of Domesticity, 1840–1870," *Journal of Interdisciplinary History,* vol. 7, no. 1 (Summer 1976), pp. 33–56; and Kenneth L. Ames, "Meaning in Artifacts: Hall Furnishings in Victorian America," *Journal of Interdisciplinary History,* vol. 9, no. 1 (Summer 1978), pp. 19–46.

30. See Haller and Haller, *Physician and Sexuality,* pp. 92–96.

31. See Marion Harland, *Eve's Daughters; or, Common Sense for the Maid, Wife, and Mother* (New York: J. R. Anderson & H. S. Allen, 1882), p. 77; and Emma Drake, *What a Young Wife Ought to Know* (Philadelphia: Vir Publishing Co., 1908), pp. 87–90 (see also Haller and Haller, *Physician and Sexuality,* pp. 124–31); Delos Wilcox, *Ethical Marriage* (Michigan, 1900), pp. 137–39 (quoted in Haller and Haller, p. 130); Mary Wood-Allen, *Marriage: Its Duties and Privileges* (Chicago: F. H. Revell, 1901), p. 194.

32. Wood-Allen, *What a Young Wife Ought to Know,* pp. 152, 157.

33. Drake, *What a Young Wife Ought to Know,* pp. 87–88; Sylvester Graham, *A Lecture to Young Men on Chastity, Intended for the Serious Consideration of Parents and Guardians* (Boston: George W. Light, 1839), p. 83. See also Siegfried Giedion, *Mechanization Takes Command* (New York: W. W. Norton & Co., 1969), pp. 201–8.

34. Elizabeth F. Holt, *From Attic to Cellar* (Salem, Mass.: The Salem Press, 1892), pp. 11–12.

35. Wood-Allen, *Marriage,* p. 49; Sylvanus Stall, *What Every Young Man Ought to Know* (Philadelphia: Vir Publishing Co., 1897), p. 241.

36. Elizabeth Blackwell, *The Human Element in Sex; Being a Medical Enquiry into the Relation of Sexual Physiology to Christian Morality* (London: Cassell & Co., 1884).

37. Wood-Allen, *What a Young Woman Ought to Know,* pp. 48, 55–68, 43.

38. See Foucault, *Madness and Civilization.*

39. "Bed-Rooms and Beds," *The Household,* vol. 7, no. 1 (January 1874), p. 4. Mrs. E. G. Cook, M.D., "The Necessity for Ventilation," *Demorest's,* vol. 23, no. 12 (October 1887), pp. 775, 774.

40. "Air-Famine," *Good Housekeeping,* vol. 9, no. 7 (3 August 1889), p. 150; *The Household,* vol. 12, nos. 3–6 (March–June 1889); "Fifteen Rules for the Preservation of Health," *Godey's,* vol. 61 (October 1860), p. 364.

41. *Bazar-Book of Decorum,* p. 24; "Be Always Neat," *The Household,* vol. 7, no. 1 (January 1874), p. 2; Wood-Allen, *What a Young Woman Ought to Know,* pp. 80–81, 79–80.

42. Mrs. E. G. Cook, M.D., "Sanitarian," *Demorest's,* vol. 23, no. 11 (September 1887), pp. 715–16; John H. Kellogg, *The Hygienic Cook-Book* (Battle Creek, Mich.: Office of the Health Reformer, 1875), p. 24. Victorian women's magazines were full of kitchen hints, recipes, and guides for more healthful fare. See, for example, "Hints About Food," *The Household,* vol. 12, no. 3 (March 1879), p. 56; Anna Holyoke, "The Arithmetic Cure," *The Household,* vol. 13, no. 2 (February 1880), p. 40.

43. "The Art of Cookery," *Godey's,* vol. 92, no. 547 (January 1876), p. 91; Cook, "Sanitarian," pp. 715–16.

44. George Beard, *American Nervousness: Its Causes and Consequences* (New York: G. P. Putnam's Sons, 1881), pp. 126, 131.

45. Beard, *American Nervousness,* p. 26. See also "The Rest Needed by Head-Workers," *The Household,* vol. 13, no. 12 (December 1880), p. 270.

46. See Haller and Haller, *Physician and Sexuality,* pp. 8–9.

47. George Beard, *Eating and Drinking: A Popular Manual of Food and Diet on Health and Disease* (New York: G. P. Putnam's Sons, 1871), p. 103; [Arabella Kenealy, M.D.], "A Lady Doctor on the Girl of Today," *Medical Record,* vol. 55 (1899), p. 719.

48. Moses T. Runnells, "Physical Degeneracy of American Women," *Medical Era,* vol. 3 (1886), pp. 302–3.

49. G. M. Hammond, "Nerves and the American Woman," *Harpers Bazaar,* vol. 40 (1906), pp. 592–93; William A. Hammond, *Cerebral Hyperaemia; the Result of Mental Strain or Emotional Disturbance; the So-Called Nervous Prostration or Neurasthenia* (New York: G. P. Putnam's Sons, 1895), pp. 70–71.

50. Hugh Campbell, *A Treatise on Nervous Exhaustion and Diseases Caused by It* (London: H. Renshaw, 1874), pp. 6, 9.

51. Shepard and Dudley, *Descriptive Catalog of Apparatus for Deformities and Deficiences, Elastic Stockings, Galvanic Batteries, Inhalation Appliances, etc. etc.* (New York, c. 1880), pp. 112–13, 116–20.

52. The best history of the patent medicine business in the nineteenth century is James Harvey Young, *The Toadstool Millionaires* (Princeton, N.J.: Princeton University Press, 1961). See also "The Alcohol in Secret Nostrums," *Medical World, vol.* 13 (1904), p. 288; Haller and Haller, *Physician and Sexuality,* pp. 288–89.

53. Haller and Haller, *Physician and Sexuality,* pp. 275–86. See also F. E. Oliver, "The Use and Abuse of Opium," *Report of the State Board of Health of Boston III* (1872); O. Marshall, "The Opium Habit in Michigan," *Report of the Board of Health of Lansing VI* (1878); E. W. Shipman, "The Promiscuous Use of Opium in Vermont," *Transactions of Vermont State Medical Society* (1890); G. W. Stone, "Opiates and Ethics," *Transactions of Kentucky State Medical Society VIII* (1900).

54. Kellog, *Household Manual,* p. 103.

55. Wood-Allen, *What a Young Woman Ought to Know,* p. 232.

56. Charles P. Uhle, M.D., "Hysteria," *Godey's,* vol. 81, no. 483 (September 1870), pp. 279–80. See also Carroll Smith-Rosenberg, "The Hysterical Woman: Sex Roles and Role Conflict in

Nineteenth-Century America," *Social Research,* vol. 39 (Winter 1972), pp. 652–78; and David J. Rothman, *The Discovery of the Asylum* (Boston: Beacon Press, 1970).

57. Uhle, "Hysteria," p. 280.

58. Ibid.

CHAPTER SIX. CYCLING AND SOCIAL GRACES

1. Diaries of Almira D. MacDonald, 22 July 1870, Margaret Woodbury Strong Museum, Rochester, N.Y.

2. Florence M. Hall, *The Correct Thing in Good Society* (Boston: D. Estes & Co., 1888), p. 35.

3. S. L. Louis, *Decorum: A Practical Treatise on Etiquette and Dress* (New York: Union Publishing Co., 1882), p. 84. See also Kenneth Ames, "Meaning in Artifacts: Hall Furnishings in Victorian America," *Journal of Interdisciplinary History,* vol. 9, no. 1 (Summer 1978), p. 42.

4. Anthea Callen, *Women Artists of the Arts and Craft Movement 1870–1914* (New York: Pantheon Books, 1979), p. 219.

5. *The Household,* vol. 15, no. 4 (April 1882), p. 97.

6. Dee Garrison, "Immoral Fiction in the Late Victorian Library," *American Quarterly,* vol. 28 (Spring 1976), pp. 71–89. See also United States Bureau of Education, *Public Libraries in the United States of America, Their History, Condition, and Management. Special Report, Part I* (Washington, D.C.: Government Printing Office, 1876), p. 393.

7. Rhoda Broughton, *Belinda* (London: Richard Bentley & Son, 1883).

8. Diaries of Almira MacDonald, 3, 6, and 9 December 1895.

9. Catherine Beecher, *Miss Beecher's Housekeeper and Healthkeeper* (New York: Harper & Brothers, 1874), p. 299.

10. *Godey's Lady's Book and Magazine,* vol. 117, no. 694 (April 1888), pp. 338–39.

11. S. D. Kehoe, *The Indian Club Exercises* (New York: Peck & Snyder, 1866), p. 71.

12. Foster R. Dulles, *A History of Recreation* (New York: Appleton-Century-Crofts, 1965), pp. 193–265.

13. *Harper's Weekly,* vol. 33 (1889), p. 463; quoted in Dulles, *History of Recreation,* p. 194.

14. *Godey's,* vol. 117, no. 697 (July 1888), p. 68.

15. John S. Haller and Robin M. Haller, *The Physician and Sexuality in Victorian America* (Urbana: University of Illinois Press, 1974), p. 174.

16. Genevieve Hecker, *Golf for Women* (New York: Peck & Snyder, 1902), pp. 19–20, 23.

17. *Godey's,* vol. 117, no. 695 (May 1888), p. 442.

18. Ibid., p. 443.

19. Ibid., p. 443.

20. Ibid., p. 444.

21. Thomas Lothrop and William Potter, "Women and the Bicycle," *Buffalo Medical Journal,* vol. 35 (1896), pp. 348–49; Maria E. Ward, *Bicycling for Ladies* (New York: Brentano's, 1896), p. 13.

22. Robert A. Smith, *A Social History of the Bicycle* (New York: American Heritage Press, 1972), pp. 27, 116–17.

23. Ibid., p. 78.

24. M. Cooke, *Our Social Manual for All Occasions* (Chicago: H. J. Smith & Co., 1896), pp. 343–48.

25. Ibid., p. 29; *Godey's,* vol. 116, no. 692 (February 1888), p. 188; *Godey's,* vol. 116, no. 693 (March 1888), p. 210; Ward, *Bicycling,* p. 27; Cooke, *Our Social Manual,* pp. 349–50; Ward, *Bicycling,* p. 53.

26. *Godey's,* vol. 116, no. 694 (April 1888), p. 391.

CHAPTER SEVEN. A HOME IN HEAVEN

1. Diaries of Almira D. MacDonald, 1870, 1885, Margaret Woodbury Strong Museum, Rochester, N.Y.

2. Alcesta Huntington to Annjenett Huntington, 14 December 1867, Huntington-Hooker Papers; Diaries of Carolyn T. Lyon, 1897, 1901, Carolyn

T. Lyon Papers, University of Rochester, Rochester, N.Y. Alcesta Huntington to Annjenett Huntington, 25 January 1868, and Susan Hooker to Alcesta Huntington, 18 April 1869, Huntington-Hooker Papers, University of Rochester, Rochester, N.Y.

3. See Charles Rosenberg, *The Cholera Years: The United States in 1832, 1849, and 1866* (Chicago: University of Chicago Press, 1962); "Death Rate by Sex and Selected Causes, Massachusetts, 1860–1970," *Historical Statistics of the United States* (Washington, D.C.: Government Printing Office, 1976), p. 63.

4. Peter R. Uhlenberg, "A Study of Cohort Life Cycles: Cohorts of Native-Born Massachusetts Women, 1830–1920," *Population Studies,* vol. 23, pp. 407–8.

5. "Expectation of Life at Specified Ages, by Sex, for Massachusetts: 1850 to 1949–51," *Historical Statistics of the United States,* p. 63.

6. Of all Massachusetts mothers born in 1850 26% died before they were fifty-five; 22% of those born in 1870 died before they had attained that age; 5.6% of the mothers born in 1920 had died by 1975. Uhlenberg, "A Study of Cohort Life Cycles," pp. 410, 412–15.

7. Mary Wood-Allen, *What a Young Girl Ought to Know* (Philadelphia: Vir Publishing Co., 1905), p. 32.

8. Augusta Moore, ed., *Notes From Plimouth Pulpit: A Collection of Memorable Passages from the Discourses of Henry Ward Beecher* (New York: Derby & Jackson, 1859), p. 47; Henry Ward Beecher, *Royal Truths* (Boston: Ticknor & Fields, 1866), pp. 232–33.

9. M. E. S., "Imprisoned," *Godey's Lady's Book and Magazine,* vol. 87, no. 521 (November 1873), p. 421.

10. "Chitchat," *Godey's,* vol. 86, no. 513 (March 1873), p. 293.

11. Ann Douglas, *The Feminization of American Culture* (New York: Alfred A. Knopf, 1978), p.

22. For an excellent study of women and evangelicalism, see Barbara Leslie Epstein, *The Politics of Domesticity* (Middletown, Conn.: Wesleyan University Press, 1981). See also Timothy Smith, *Revivalism and Social Reform* (New York: Harper & Row, 1957), pp. 20–21; Stow Persons, "Religion and Modernity, 1865–1914," in James Ward Smith and A. Leland Jamison, eds., *The Shaping of American Religion* (Princeton, N.J.: Princeton University Press, 1961), pp. 369–401.

12. "Questions of Importance," *Godey's,* vol. 80, no. 477 (March 1870), p. 286.

13. "Timothy Titcomb" [Josiah Gilbert Holland], *Titcomb's Letters to Young People, Single and Married* (New York: Charles Scribner, 1858), pp. 155–57.

14. Ibid., pp. 161–62. For a provocative discussion of the interrelationship of women and ministers, see Douglas, *Feminization of American Culture.*

15. Reverend R. P. Roe, Preface to *From Jest to Earnest* (New York: Dodd, Mead & Co., 1875).

16. A best-seller is defined as any work whose volume of sales is equal to one percent of the population. For sales figures, see James D. Hart, *The Popular Book* (Berkeley: University of California Press, 1950). The best studies of the religious novel in America are Willard Thorp, "The Religious Novel as Best-Seller in America," in James Ward Smith and A. Leland Jamison, eds., *Religious Perspectives in American Culture* (Princeton, N.J.: Princeton University Press, 1961), pp. 195–241; and Herbert Ross Brown, *The Sentimental Novel in America* (Durham, N.C.: Duke University Press, 1940), chap. 5.

17. Thorp, "The Religious Novel as Best-Seller," pp. 200–1; *Books in Print, 1980–81* (New York: R. R. Bowker Co., 1980), p. 2022.

18. Douglas, *Feminization of American Culture,* pp. 107–8; Thorp, "Religious Novel as Best-Seller," pp. 214–16.

19. Mary F. Tucker, "Going," *The Lady's Friend,* vol. 7, no. 5 (May 1870), p. 317.

20. The figures for *Godey's* are: 1870, 39.4%; 1838, 44.7%; 1878, 39.0%; 1883, 41.4%; 1888, 40.7%; 1893, 41.4%.

21. Eben E. Rexford, "Row Me Over," *The Lady's Friend,* vol. 7, no. 3 (March 1870), p. 177.

22. Elizabeth Stuart Phelps, *Songs of the Silent World* (Boston: Houghton Mifflin Co., 1885), p. 112.

23. See, for example, James J. Farrell, *Inventing the American Way of Death, 1830–1920* (Philadelphia: Temple University Press, 1980); David O. Stannard, ed., *Death in America* (Philadelphia: University of Pennsylvania Press, 1975); Lawrence Taylor, "Symbolic Death: An Anthropological View of Mourning Ritual in the Nineteenth Century," in Martha V. Pike and Janice G. Armstrong, eds., *A Time to Mourn* (Stony Brook, N.Y.: Museums at Stony Brook, 1980), pp. 39–48.

Cox, Palmer, 55
croquet, 152

dances and balls, 13–14
Darwin, Charles, 8, 122
death and mourning, 165–79; burial procedures and funerals, 167–8, 179; child mortality, 166; child-bearing and life expectancy, 166–7, 198 *n*. 6; clothes, jewelry, decorative devices, 170–3; flow-ers, 172–3; illness, epidemics, mortality rates, 165–6; literature of consolation, 177–9; male *vs.* female mortality rates, 165; men, etiquette for, 173; mourning period and prescribed behavior, 170, 171–2; stationery for, 172, 173
decoration, home, 93–111; bathroom, 104–5; bed-chamber, 102–4; dining room, 100–2; entrance hall, 94–6; floor coverings, 105–6; furniture cov-ers, 98–9; and garden/sanctuary ideology, 36–7; hearth, 98; "ideal" home, 93; information sources, 94; kitchen, 102; parlor or drawing room, 96–8, 195 *n*. 29; style, general, 93–4; textiles, 99–100, 101; wall decoration, 107–10; for weddings, 24–5; window dressings, 106–7; window shades, 110. *See also* housework
Demorest's Monthly Magazine, 18, 29, 41, 42, 113–14, 117, 134, 135, 140, 177
DeMund, Mary Wilcox, 187 *n*. 27
Deterioration of the Puritan Stock and Its Causes (Ellis), 16–17
Diet After Weaning (Mellin Food Company), 40, 46–7
diet and feeding practices, childrearing and, 38, 39; weaning and, 40–2
dining room, decoration of, 100–2
diphtheria, 165
Domestic Receipt Book (C. Beecher), 87
domestics: decline in availability, 86–7; pay scales, 190 *n*. 21; training, employer relationships and, 88–91
Drake, Emma, 119, 131, 132
Dress-Reform (essays), 124–5
drugs, women as primary users of, 38, 140–1
Dudden, Faye, 87
Dwight, Theodore, 35
dyspepsia (indigestion), 135–6

Eastlake, Charles Locke (*also* Eastlake Style), 84, 102, 107
Eating and Drinking . . . Disease (Beard), 137, 138
Edis, Robert, 103
education: of children, 45–6; as leisure activity, 149–50
Ellis, John, 16–17
embroidery, home decoration and, 100, 101
engagements. *See* courtship; marriage
entrance hall, decoration of, 94–6
étagères, 96–7
Ethics of Marriage (Pomeroy), 29
Everett, Edward, 7
Eve's Daughter . . . and Mother (Harland), 131
exercise, 150–1; as cure-all, 136. *See also names of activities and sports*

fashion. *See* physical health
Father's Book, The (Dwight), 35
fireplaces, 98
fishing, 158, 159
flirting, 12
floor coverings, 105–6
Fowler, Orson S., 118, 120–1
Frank Leslie's Illustrated Magazine, 129
From Attic to Cellar (Holt), 70
From Jest to Earnest (Roe), 176
fruit preservation (drying, canning, etc.), 62–6
funerals. *See* death and mourning
furniture, gender-defined style in, 97–8. *See also* home decoration

Gates Ajar, The (Phelps), 148, 167
Gayworthy's, The (Whitney), 177
Gentle Measures in the Management and Training of Children (Jacob Abbott), 35
Gentry, Thomas, 56
George, H. Maria, 53
Gibson, Charles Dana (*also* Gibson style), 115, 117
gifts: courtship, 14–15, 16; wedding, 22–4
Gill, Thomas P., 184
Gilman, Charlotte Perkins, 36

One...Two...Three...
SASSAFRAS!

by Stuart J. Murphy · illustrated by John Wallace

HarperCollins*Publishers*

Epb
Murphy

To Madeleine Grace—with her smiley face!
—S.J.M.

To Zach, Jake, and A.J.
—J.W.

The publisher and author would like to thank teachers Patricia Chase, Phyllis Goldman, and Patrick Hopfensperger for their help in making the math in MathStart just right for kids.

HarperCollins®, ☰®, and MathStart® are registered trademarks of HarperCollins Publishers. For more information about the MathStart series, write to HarperCollins Children's Books, 1350 Avenue of the Americas, New York, NY 10019, or visit our website at www.mathstartbooks.com.

Bugs incorporated in the MathStart series design were painted by Jon Buller.

One . . . Two . . . Three . . . Sassafras!
Text copyright © 2002 by Stuart J. Murphy
Illustrations copyright © 2002 by John Wallace

Library of Congress Cataloging-in-Publication Data
Murphy, Stuart J.
    One . . . two . . . three . . . sassafras! / by Stuart J. Murphy ; illustrated by John Wallace.
        p.   cm. — (MathStart)
"Number order."
"Level 1."
Summary: At a family reunion, the cousins line up in order of their ages to get their pictures taken, introducing the concept of numerical order.
ISBN 0-06-028916-3 — ISBN 0-06-028917-1 (lib. bdg.) — ISBN 0-06-446246-3 (pbk.)
1. Sequences (Mathematics)—Juvenile literature.   [1. Sequences (Mathematics)]   I. Wallace, John, ill.   II. Title.   III. Series.
QA246.5.M875   2002   00-054033
515'.24—dc21

Typography by Elynn Cohen   1 2 3 4 5 6 7 8 9 10   ❖   First Edition

One...Two...Three... SASSAFRAS!

Uncle Howie always took the photos at the Lumpkin family reunions. He had a camera that developed the pictures right away.

4

This year he took pictures
of Grandma Zelda dancing
the tango,

Aunt Bertha tasting the
frosting on the cake,

and Uncle Morris's wig
falling into the punch.

5

And then it was time for pictures of all the cousins.

"Sally! Max! David!" Uncle Howie yelled. "Come and line up for your picture."

6

The 3 cousins came running over.

"Where's Bonzo?" Sally said. "We can't take a picture without Bonzo!"

"There's no cousin Bonzo!" said Uncle Howie. But Sally didn't hear.

"Bonzo!" called Sally. "Where are you?"

"Line up from youngest to oldest," said Uncle Howie.

"I'm 6," said Max.

"I'm 9," said Sally.

"I just turned 8," said David. "So I go in between."

Max
6

David
8

Sally
9

"Say, 'Sassafras!'" said Uncle Howie.

"SASSAFRAS!" Max and David yelled.

"Bonzo!" Sally shouted. "There you are!"

And she ran away just before Uncle Howie pressed the button. "Fiddlesticks!" Uncle Howie exclaimed. "The picture's ruined!"

Adam and Briana came to look. "Is it our turn?" asked Briana.

"I'll take all 4 of you together," said Uncle Howie. "Line up from youngest to oldest."

"I'm 11," said Adam. "I'll get over here on the end."

"I'm almost 8," said Briana. "And I want to be next to Adam."

"No way," said David, as he pushed himself between Briana and Adam. "Almost 8 is still only 7."

Max
6

David
8

Briana
7

Adam
11

Max
6

Briana
7

David
8

Adam
11

They were finally ready.

"Say, 'Sassafras!'" Uncle Howie said.

"SASSAFRAS!" they all shouted. But just before Uncle Howie pressed the button, Briana poked David, and David bumped into Adam.

"Jumping jelly beans!" exclaimed Uncle Howie. "The picture's ruined!"

Max
6

Briana
7

David
8

Adam
11

Tanya and Leticia walked by with Jacob in his stroller.

"Are you ready for us?" Tanya asked.

"I'll take you all together," said Uncle Howie. "Line up from youngest to oldest."

"I'm 15," said Tanya. She was definitely the oldest.

Max
6

Briana
7

David
8

"I'm 13," said Leticia, "but Adam's a lot taller than me.
I'll get between David and him."

Jacob
1

Leticia
13

Adam
11

Tanya
15

"No, no, no!" said Uncle Howie. "Try again!"

"I'm only 11," said Adam to Leticia. "You go between Tanya and me."

"And Jacob belongs down here, next to Max," said Briana.

Jacob
1

Max
6

Briana
7

David
8

Leticia tried to stand on tiptoe so she would be as tall as Adam.

Adam
11

Leticia
13

Tanya
15

"Say, 'Sassafras!'" said Uncle Howie.

"SASSAFRAS!" everyone shouted.

But just before Uncle Howie pressed the button, Jacob dropped his teddy bear, David poked Briana back, and Leticia couldn't stand on her tiptoes any longer.

"Great galloping gillywhoppers!" Uncle Howie exclaimed. "The picture's ruined!"

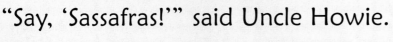

"That's it!" said Uncle Howie. "I only have 1 more picture. It has to have everybody in it. Nobody cry. Nobody fall down. And everybody say, 'Sassafras!'"

"Wait! Where's Sally?" Adam asked. "She's the only cousin who's not here!"

"Sally!" everybody yelled.

25

Sally ran over. But she didn't look happy.

"I can't find Bonzo!" she said. "We can't have a family picture without Bonzo!"

"There IS no cousin Bonzo!" Uncle Howie shouted. "Now everybody get in line!"

Jacob
1

Max
6

Briana
7

David
8

"Sally, you're 9, so get between David and me,"
Adam said.

Sally
9

Adam
11

Leticia
13

Tanya
15

"One . . . two . . . three . . . Sassafras!" said Uncle Howie.
"And, Sally, smile!"

Sassafras!

everybody yelled.
Except Sally.

Sally shouted.

29

Just before Uncle Howie pressed the
button, Bonzo jumped right into Sally's arms.
Uncle Howie was speechless.
"Bonzo!" said Sally. "You're in the picture, too!"

In *One . . . Two . . . Three . . . Sassafras!* the math concept is arranging numbers in order. This concept helps in the development of number sense and enhances counting skills. It also prepares children to understand place value.

If you would like to have more fun with the math concepts presented in *One . . . Two . . . Three . . . Sassafras!* here are a few suggestions:

• Read the story with the child and discuss how Uncle Howie has the children line up by age before he takes a picture.

• There are several ways that the children in the story could have been arranged by Uncle Howie—for example, by height or alphabetically by name. Help the child explore various other possibilities.

• Have the child draw pictures of his or her family. Cut out the drawings and have the child arrange them by age from youngest to oldest.

• Write the numbers 1 through 15 on separate index cards. Mix the cards and remove one from the pile without letting the child see which card you have taken. Then have him or her figure out which card is missing.

• When you count by ones, there is a pattern to the order of the numbers. For example, 3 is one more than 2, and 4 is one more than 3. Discuss this with the child and see if he or she can figure out that each number is always one more than the previous number.

Following are some activities that will help you extend the concepts presented in *One . . . Two . . . Three . . . Sassafras!* into a child's everyday life:

Toy Lineup: Have the child pick 1 toy (for example, 1 teddy bear), then 2 of another toy (for example, 2 dolls), then 5 of another toy (for example, 5 blocks), and so on with whatever numbers you prefer. Then work together to put the piles of toys in order from least to greatest.

Card Game: Take a deck of cards and put aside the tens and the face cards. Each player is dealt 2 cards, which he or she uses to make a 2-digit number. (For example, a player who is dealt an ace and a 9 can make 19 or 91.) The players place their numbers in order. The person with the smallest number collects all the cards. After all the cards have been played, the player with the most cards wins.

Sports: Find the jersey numbers of the players for the child's favorite sports team. These can be found in the newspaper, the team's website, or a program from a game. Have the child place the players in order using the numbers on their jerseys.

The following books include concepts similar to those that are presented in *One . . . Two . . . Three . . . Sassafras!*

- NUMBERS by Richard L. Allington

- ME FIRST by Helen Lester

- THE ROBBERS FIVE OR IS IT SIX? by Maria Van Eeden

ABOUT THE AUTHOR

Harvey Green was born in Buffalo, New York. He received a B.A. from the University of Rochester, an M.A. and a Ph.D. from Rutgers University, and a second M.A. from the Cooperstown Graduate Programs in History Museum Studies. He is the historian at the Margaret Woodbury Strong Museum in Rochester, New York. The Strong Museum, which opened its doors to the public in 1982, is a history museum that houses one of the world's largest collections of Victorian materials. It is the only major national museum devoted entirely to documenting life in Victorian America. For the past six years, Harvey Green has worked on interpreting the 300,000 objects collected by Margaret Woodbury Strong, an heiress to the Kodak fortune, and on organizing the museum's opening exhibits, including "The Light of the Home: Middle Class American Women, 1870–1910."

Mary-Ellen Perry is curator of fine arts at the Strong Museum, and principal curator of the exhibit "The Light of the Home."